HOLLY

A TREE FOR ALL SEASONS

Chris Howkins

Published by
Chris Howkins

1

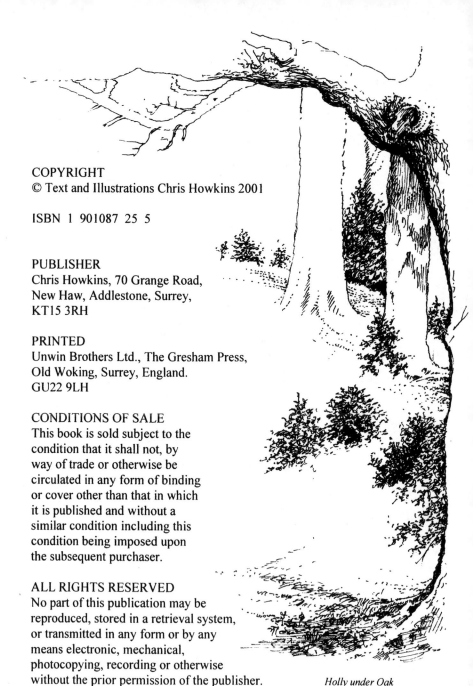

PUBLISHER
Chris Howkins, 70 Grange Road,
New Haw, Addlestone, Surrey,
KT15 3RH

PRINTED
Unwin Brothers Ltd., The Gresham Press,
Old Woking, Surrey, England.
GU22 9LH

Holly under Oak

CONTENTS

PART ONE - THE RITUAL USES

PART TWO - THE PRACTICAL USES

INTRODUCTION

Each autumn, as the nights begin to 'draw in' and we 'put the clocks back', so little sprigs of Holly start to appear on all the merchandising. Christmas is coming. More pertinently, the end of the year is coming, for Holly was used as a ritual plant at this season for thousands of years before the coming of Christianity. Now, in a multi-cultural society, it's become a generalised commercial symbol, making Holly one of our best known trees. This long association with mankind has given it a fascinating social history, both in ritual and practical uses, and this distinction has been retained in the two sections of this book. Much of the ritual usage has to remain conjectural and, fascinating as the varying views may be, this is not the place to explore them. This is only an introduction, which will no doubt get modified again and again in the light of further historical reviews and archaeological exploration. Even the practical uses are poorly documented. They are also difficult to group together for the purposes of this book. For example, it would seem sensible to put all block-makers together, whether for book illustration, cotton textile printing or wallpaper designs. However, that then separates the Holly's other important use in the cotton mills, for making the bobbins, and what happens then to weavers' shuttles from the woollen textile industry? The other problem, as usual, is deciding how far to explore the social history themes once introduced. Readers will find the introductions do not proceed very far but significant dates and names are given to aid further reading.

SOURCES

This book is only an introduction to the Holly tree. Many of the subjects and themes are themselves part of much broader issues, ranging from the developments in Christianity through to the cotton industry in the Industrial Revolution. Each of these main themes offers much more to the reader than can be presented here. This is particularly so for the ritual uses, with all the varying interpretations of the evidence, which made the footnotes far too extensive for an introduction of this nature. Readers are therefore directed to the extensive notes and bibliographies in two recent publications: for the origins of Christianity to *The Jesus Mysteries* by Timothy Freke and Peter Gandy, and for its application in Britain to *The Stations of the Sun* by Ronald Hutton. These and other texts, especially for the practical uses, are listed in the final bibliography.

ACKNOWLEDGEMENTS

Much of the content has been drawn from material gathered over the last thirty years and thanks are due to all the many people who have contributed to that database. In particular, thanks are due to the craftsmen and historians who work with the tree or its history today, for their invaluable help in verifying or contradicting statements made in earlier publications. In particular there was a problem over contradictory statements as to whether or not the Native Americans had knowledge of birdlime *before* the Europeans arrived. Technologically, the most advanced of those peoples at the time were the Cherokee Nations and I am most indebted to Michael (Aquah) Johnson, of the Cherokee Blue (Holly) clan for all his service in directing my enquiries through the learned elders of the Nations. There is no definitive answer at the time of going to print. Enquiries with other Nations have not been pursued; sources such as the Iroquois Museum replied simply, "We have no answer for you."

For translating 17th/18th century French thanks are due to Liz. Willis, and to Brian Rich for material from the North Midlands and Northern England. Help with research, proof reading and final page setting given by Sue Harvey, Nick Sampson, Gordon Weaver, Stuart Salt, and Aaron Mason.

WHICH HOLLY ?

The little sprigs of Holly that are used as a seasonal symbol at Christmastime ensure that its leaves and berries are widely known. However, there are many different Hollies throughout the world, although they are not well represented in Africa and Australia. Exactly how many is disputed. Older books[1] say nearly two hundred whereas later texts[2], in the light of further study, say over four hundred. They are very varied and not all of them are trees, for some are shrubs, climbers and even epiphytes. Some are deciduous while others are evergreen. The Holly featured in this study is the European evergreen tree *Ilex aquifolium* L.

Today it grows naturally in North West Europe from Norway across to North West and Southern Germany, and southwards to the Mediterranean where it then becomes restricted to the cooler mountainous regions. Its range is determined by its bark. This is thin and smooth so it does not provide enough frost protection for cambium cells beneath. Similarly, without deep fissures to cast cooler shadows ultra violet rays of strong sunshine can penetrate and kill. Thus the Holly tends to be a woodland tree so that it can benefit from the protection afforded by the other trees. When growing away from these the Holly develops drooping branches that, under ideal conditions, swish a full skirt of protective foliage all round down to ground level. The tree's tolerance of cold is so precisely limited that it can be used as a prehistoric climatic indicator. It shows, for example, that during the Pleistocene period the summer temperature was about 2°C higher than today's average. Winters were warmer too[3]. Thus the tree disappears from the record during the Ice Ages. During this current interglacial the Holly returned about 9,000 years ago.

As for size, the Holly is not among our tallest trees but nevertheless it can reach heights of about eighty feet. In girth it reaches eight or nine feet. There are some wonderful short bulky-trunked ones where the trees have been pollarded and with increasing age they become hollow. Some in the Forest of Dean (Glos.) have parts of their cylinder wall of trunk decayed through in places, leaving the trunk seemingly stilted on legs, looking eerie in the failing light. Back in 1657 William Coles recorded the following anecdote in his *Adam in Eden*:-

> *One that I know had a Holly Tree growing in his Orchard of that bignesse that being cut down he caused it to be sawn out in boards, and made himselfe thereof a Coffin, and if I mistake not left enough to make his wife one also. But the parties were very corpulent, and therefore you may imagine that the Tree could not be small.*

---

[1] e.g. Brimble, L. J. F; *Trees in Britain*; Macmillan; 1948
[2] e.g. Royal Horticultural Society; *Dictionary of Gardening*; Macmillan; 1992
[3] see Godwin for details of prehistory; thermal distribution maps pp. 172-5

Most familiar are the smaller shrubby youngsters that grow under other trees in woodlands, especially under oaks. There the light is poor which reduces their capacity to make food. By way of compensation the leaves are charged with extra quantities of green chlorophyll that is essential for the process. That's why Holly leaves are such a dark green. They are shiny with their waterproofing oils, which also reduce evapotranspiration, enabling it to survive both summer drought under the trees and winter frosts that freeze the ground water. In severe winter weather Hollies have been known to shed their leaves to terminate further water loss. Those oils are also what make green Holly burn so fiercely which can be a severe disadvantage in forest fires. That surface cuticle of the leaf is thicker than for many plants, having two or more layers of cells.[4] Around the edges the leaves develop a sort of hem of fused sclerotic (hardening) cells to keep the margin intact and that is drawn out into the spines.[5]

Before the familiar berries, the mature twigs sprout cymes of white flowers from the leaf axils. Where the leaves are close together this gives the effect of the twigs being wreathed along their length with the white blossom. This occurs

---

[4] Lowson, p.148
[5] Bower, pp. 189-90

usually in May but can be found as late as August, depending upon the genetic strain of the specimen. Early bloomers often have some of the previous year's berries still on the twigs, (although this depends whether the wildlife has needed them as food in hard winters). The notion that male and female flowers are on separate trees is well known but not always so; hermaphrodites do occur.

Quercus ilex

THE HOLLY OAK

In the history of the ritual use of evergreens in the eastern Mediterranean there are areas where the Holly does not grow. There, the Holly Oak, *Quercus ilex*, was used instead. This is the tree that gave its name to the genus *Ilex*. It does not grow naturally in Britain but was introduced about 1500. It's been popular for seaside plantings, especially in the South and South West, for being salt resistant, and can be found else-where in parks and gardens. The longest avenue of these trees in Europe is in Britain at Goring-by-Sea, West Sussex. It stretches seven eighths of a mile and has some 450 specimens, including some young ones, thereby showing its stages of development.[6] Other English names are Holm Oak and Evergreen Oak. As far as the ritual uses in Britain are concerned, references to Holly in this book are to *Ilex aquifolium*.

---

[6] inf. courtesy of the avenue's local conservators, *The Ilex Group*. To locate the trees find the road called 'Ilex Avenue'.

8

THE SEASONAL SYMBOL

The essential quality that has brought Holly such long lasting and international renown is its evergreen nature. Since its leaves do not die and fall off at the end of the year it seems to defy death. Therefore, it is used symbolically to carry the fertility of the old year over into the New Year.

Long, long ago, in the cultures of the Middle East, there was concern towards the end of the year that the sun was dying. Each day it climbed less high in the sky, burned less brightly, less hotly. Soon, it was concluded, the world would end in total darkness and coldness. So vital rituals were performed to revive the sun. The Babylonians, for example, turned to their powerful god Marduke and beseeched him to fight in the skies, on their behalf, a great battle between light and darkness. They lent a hand down on earth by lighting great fires, to inspire the sun's recovery. It was a sort of rallying insult: "If our fire can burn this brightly and hotly why can't you?" The sun was duly miffed and began to show people its real power. A new year was born.

To the Babylonians, Marduke was the Lord of Life, having created all living things once he had won control over the land after Tiamat (the sea) had given birth to it. He also organised the heavens and thus in this context we see him as responsible for the sun and for the growing of the crops. Additionally, he was the god to whom everyone turned in times of doubt or trouble because he had once bargained for the right to make the ultimate decisions over each person's fate.

Thus Marduke was very much the centre of attention at this time. Included in the rituals performed by the people was the hanging up of evergreens. Again, it can be viewed as an insult to the deciduous and dormant plants: "If these evergreens can keep growing through the winter, why can't you?" It worked! The sap rose, the buds swelled and the bulbs sprouted through the soil. Another spring was born. We still appreciate a cheering reassurance that spring is coming so we force bulbs, such as Hyacinths and Paperwhite Narcissi, into bloom for Christmas. We also give presents, just as did the Babylonians when they mirrored the gift of a new year from Marduke.

Narcissus

THE ROMANS

The Babylonians were just one culture among many that had this sort of seasonal ritual. The Romans were another. Their story is not so simple, since their era covers such a wide span of time, during which there were inevitable changes. Furthermore, with the development of the Empire, they encountered an increasingly wide range of other cultures (involving the use of evergreens like the Holly) and these caused further adjustments. Of course the deities had to be Romanised. Those they encountered that were associated with the sun became subsumed under the Romans' great sun god, Apollo. Not surprisingly, it is thought that Apollo's sacred tree was the Holly.

Emperor Aurelian saw that by adopting officially the Assyrian/Babylonian beliefs, which were spreading into the Western Roman Empire, he could help unify some of the disparity. Thus in 274 he declared a new public holiday for the *Dies Natalis Invicti Solis*– the Birthday of the Unconquered Sun.[7] This was a monotheistic version of sun worship, originally from Syria. On this occasion the Romans remembered that Jupiter had banished his father Saturn out into the countryside to be a minor god of agriculture but Saturn had no intention of being a minor god of anything and rose to a crucial position in control of the crops and harvests. This is all allegory. Saturn means time and he consumed all his children except Jupiter (air), Neptune (water) and Pluto (death) that time cannot consume.

The festival became the all-important Saturnalia, with the main religious rites on the 17th December, although festivities were sanctioned to the 19th, extended later to the 23rd. It thereby took in the most important time, the time when the sun might die, the winter solstice. As a state festival it lasted only forty nine years, officially, before the emperor Constantine promoted a new cult as a unifying religion of state – Christianity. That was in 323. Thus Constantine blurred deliberately the main cults of Sol Invictus, Mithraism and Christianity in his determined efforts to achieve and maintain unity. By then, some aspects of the old pre-Christian festival, both secular and sacred, had taken such a firm hold that they persisted. There was of course the public holiday itself and one with a degree of licence over behaviour that wouldn't have been acceptable or even legal at other times. There was drinking, gambling and varying forms of theatre, including role reversal. People also gave presents, among which candles were popular little 'suns' or little seasonal bonfires. There were festive decorations to go with it all, including evergreens such as the Holly. There was much that we would recognise in essence today. There was also confusion. The early Christian leaders had to exhort the celebration of the birth of Christ - not the sun.

---

[7] Hutton. p.1

The earliest Christians crept into Roman society secretly, as an outlawed cult. Each year they were at risk of being discovered when the Saturnalia was celebrated. It was then that the traditionalists decked their homes with evergreens, to encourage Saturn to give them another year's fertility. Many Christians in the community would not have wished to do so but their undecorated houses would have been dangerously conspicuous. If they did hang up evergreens, as a disguise, then that would help explain how Holly came into Christianity.

CHOOSING A BIRTHDAY

Although Holly decorations began to be acceptable to the Christians it would have been quite some time before Holly developed its close association with Christ and in particular with His birthday. That would have been due, in part, to His birthday not being commemorated at the Holly-time of the winter solstice. It was, for example, sometimes celebrated in June, since the scriptures gave no guidance. The date varied from place to place until eventually a date in the old midwinter festival was chosen. That fulfilled the Jewish prophecies and thereby added credence to the story. It challenged the old beliefs without denouncing the enjoyable and very popular birthday celebrations. Indeed it actually extended those beliefs by teaching that instead of striving for just another *year's* fertility there was now the chance, through a belief in Jesus Christ, of being rewarded with another *lifetime*, in Paradise. It took a long time to become established, so that the first certain record of Christ's birthday being celebrated on 25th December comes from the calendar of Philocalus in 354. That was probably based upon the rituals of Rome. It took nearly 200 years longer to become accepted in Jerusalem.

"It was a custom of the pagans to celebrate on the same 25 December the birthday of the Sun, at which they kindled lights in token of festivity. In these solemnities and revelries the Christians also took part. Accordingly when the doctors of the Church perceived that the Christians had a leaning to this festival, they took counsel and resolved that the true Nativity should be solemnised on that day." Syrus, late 4thC.

December 25th was a significant choice since that was also the day when pagans celebrated the birth of several other gods born as mortal men, such as Dionysus and Mithras. The cult of Mithras was the greatest challenge, apart from Judaism, to the development of Christianity. It was a faith important to the Persians and it was Persian mercenaries that were important in the Roman legions because they were considered especially valiant. This was due to their belief that Mithras was with them, as the greatest friend of all men alive and the greatest friend of all men dead. Thus this religion travelled with the legions far and wide through the known world; visitors to the City of London can still look down into the preserved archaeological remains of its great temple of Mithras from Roman times.

Central to the story so far has been the winter solstice, seen as lasting over several days, whereas today we are more inclined to think in terms of one 'shortest' day. It would have been very difficult in early times to decide exactly which was the shortest day because the sun's path appears almost constant for several. This 'standing still' is the literal meaning of solstice. To complicate matters, the date changes through the years due to the shift of the planet on its axis. Thus December 21st, 23rd, 25th, right through to 6th January have all been the shortest day. Even now there is disparity in books and diaries as to whether it is the 21st or 23rd December, while the *Oxford English Dictionary* asserts it is the 22nd! Consequently, there was a choice when Christianity was trying to fix a date for the birth of Christ.

While Christians in the west favoured 25th December, those in the east chose 6th January. The former became official except in the Armenian Church that still celebrates on 6th January. The Western Church, by the 2nd century was using the 6th January to commemorate other events in the life of Jesus: His baptism, the miracle of changing water into wine at Cana and the miracle of the feeding of the five thousand. Eventually it was accepted generally that this should be the day reserved to commemorate the presentation of the Christ child to the gentiles – to the Magi – and this became Epiphany.[8]

Obviously this was a very busy time in the ritual year of the varying cultures of the region. One of the great cities of the time was Alexandria and there the Christians were able to establish their faith by choosing 6th January for Christ's birth since it was already a sacred day. The Alexandrians in Egypt used it for another 'virgin birth' that of Aion. There were other similarities that made conversion easier. For example, St. Epiphanius tells us the Alexandrian rituals reached their climax in an underground cell (cave) where a wooden figure of Aion was made manifest, marked with 'the sign of a cross on hands, knees and head.' From Egypt we also get the origins of the midwinter festivals lasting twelve days since it appears to have started there with the birthday celebrations of Horus, the falcon-headed god.

Thus, one way or another, the twelve days from 25th December to 6th January became one long festival. The Christian Church declared this official in 567 at the Council of Tours. As this period was already packed with non-Christian

---

[8] from the Greek word meaning to show or make manifest. Girls born on this day were often named Theophania ('manifestation of God') which gives us Tiffany today.

festivals the Church added its own alternatives, such as 23rd December for Adam and Eve, 26th for St. Stephen, 27th for John the Evangelist and 28th for Holy Innocents (the babies massacred by Herod). New Year's Day became (by 546) the day Jesus got his name and was circumcised.

NEW YEAR'S DAY

Bearing in mind that this festival period was primarily a fertility rite to carry life over into a new year we would expect great importance being attached to New Year's Day. However, that has not always been on the 1st January. The early Romans began their year on 1st March so that September and October were, as their names testify, the 7th and 8th months. In the December/January period they celebrated Janus, the two-faced god who looked back into the old year and forward into the new year, and gave his name to the month of January. We still have a duality today with the new tax year beginning in April.

From Ovid we learn that the Romans changed their calendar to make 1st January New Year's Day in 153 BC. The first three days of the year were the Kalendae which, according to Varro, derives from *calling* the people together on the first day of each month for the pontifex to inform them of the important days to remember, both secular and sacred. At this time the Romans sent each other little gifts or *strenae* accompanied with sprigs of evergreens for good luck. Fresh evergreens were hung up in the temples too, which Christians accepted and perpetuated, on the Biblical authority of the Old Testament:

"The glory of Lebanon shall come unto thee, the fir tree, the pine tree, and the box together, to beautify the place of my sanctuary."　*(Isaiah, 60, 13)*

NORTH WEST EUROPE

The Holly, as a midwinter fertility aid, in the Mediterranean and Middle East, accompanied a wide range of seasonal observances. These were brought into North West Europe by the Roman legions, traders and Christian missionaries. There they encountered existing rites of a parallel nature.

Surprisingly, very little is known for certain about the midwinter festival of the Germanic and Norse people, except that it existed and that it was important to them. Again it centred upon the sun and included the ritual use of evergreens. It also lasted twelve days, or at least it is presumed to have done so, since that is the period embodied as a holiday for servants in the laws of King Alfred the Great (r.871-899). There is a great paucity of documentary evidence for the British

Isles but the festival's importance can be deduced from the repeated denouncements from the early Christian leaders. For example, in Ireland St. Patrick condemned it as early as the 5th century. In England, St. Augustine was soon writing back to Pope Gregory I seeking guidance as to how he should respond to the evergreens. The Pope replied in 604 saying, basically, adopt them into Christianity. Thus the English were allowed their midwinter evergreens by papal authority. Subsequent popes condemned them. We still use them.

We don't even know for sure what this festival was called. From the scant evidence surviving it would seem to be simply the Midwinter festival. Bede's reference in c.730 to the English having Modranicht (Mother Night; 24th December) does not stand up too well to scrutiny and in any case is the only known use of that expression. Eventually, after several hundred years of Christian influence, we get the first reference to Christmas, in 1038, when it was written as *Cristes maessan*. This was the time of Danish kingship over England and from the Scandinavians we adopted their colloquial expression of 'Yule'. This was in widespread use in North West Europe, with variations in spelling between the cultures, but we never get a clear picture of it. The original meaning of the word is not known. It is always presumed to be pre-Christian but that is not absolutely certain, since it is not until the 12th century that the English have it in popular usage to mean Christmas. The first reference from Scotland is not until the next century.

Of course it wasn't simply a matter of Christmas usurping the solstice rituals. Embedded in all these were the celebrations for New Year's Day on 1st January. It was these that tended to persist and against which the churchmen railed, like Wulfstan, Archbishop of York, between 1005-8. His reference is to the 'sorcery' which no doubt included the 'magic' influence of the evergreens. The Church has never liked fertility rituals – it's up to God whether he blesses with fertility.

The traditions remained widespread and persistent. In the late 12th century the Bishop of Exeter was decrying *"those who keep the New Year with heathen fires"* and concerns were still voiced in the 14th and in the 15th centuries. Sadly, this store of insight is likely to be seen in black and white – pagan or Christian – whereas when viewed in its broadest context it shows it's neither. It was the folk culture of our islands, an amalgam of many influences, whereby the *reason* for the celebration was understood as Christian but the *ways* in which it was performed were drawn from the tradition of the folk culture. In many instances the celebrants wouldn't have been able to say *why* the features were included. It's still the same today. Ask shoppers why they've bought Holly and they reply, *"Because it's Christmas."*

THE HOLLY BECOMES HOLY

Despite those denouncements by early Church leaders the use of Holly and other evergreens at midwinter persisted throughout the Middle Ages and beyond. The seasonal rituals settled down into a comfortably reassuring way of doing things, with churches and homes being decorated with flowers and greenery on the most important sacred days through the year – not just at Christmas. Indeed the Church ended up with such a succession of holy days through late autumn and into winter that Christmas was just one day of many. In due course it would be banned altogether without rupturing the faith.

Angel; medieval stained glass. Leatherhead church, Surrey.

Through the Middle Ages the Holly became accepted increasingly as the appropriate plant to be held sacred to Jesus. It became the *holy* tree and many a book today asserts quite categorically that the name *holly* derives from *holy*. It does not. The two words have separate etymologies. The Saxon word for *holy* was *halig* whereas the tree was called *holen* or *holegn*.[9] These became *holin* or *hollin* and then *holm* by Chaucer's time in the 14th century. That was superseded by *holly* (during the early 1500s as a broad generalisation) until *holly* and *holy* were inextricably linked by association. This was not simply a matter of spelling for literate classes but something that was demonstrated through using the Holly in a holy way in the rituals. Apart from seeing it, people also heard it, both in church music and in popular ballads. The tree was also an item of trade with the church and there's nothing like a bit of business to fine-tune people's thinking!

---

[9] The Saxon *cneowholen* meant *knee-holly*, referring to its height. See Pollington, p.84 Sometimes it refers to Butchers' Broom, *Ruscus aculeatus*.

Continuing with the theme of the old names, some get trapped in the country names for the Mistle Thrush, which loves to feed on the berries. Thus in the south-west, from Dorset to Cornwall, the bird has been called the Holm Thrush, Holm Cock and Holm Screech. In Yorkshire it's the Hollin Cock.[10]

THE HOLLY GOES TO CHURCH

It is through trading that we gain an insight into the developing rituals. Sadly, church financial accounts from the early Middle Ages are either very rare or lost altogether but from the later Middle Ages we do have records[11] for buying the Holly, Ivy and other evergreens at Christmas. Thus from Thame in Oxfordshire in 1474-5 we find:

For tallow candell holme and Ivye agens Cristmesse....iiij d.

The practice continues in England right through the Reformation up to 1647. These purchases are sometimes listed simply as 'garnishing' or 'trimming' as in this instance from St. Mary's Cambridge in 1624-5:

For trimming the Church against Christmas....ij s. vj d.

---

[10] Lockwood, W. B.; *The Oxford Book of British Bird Names; OUP; 1984*
[11] quoted examples from Cox.

The decorative schemes were far more lavish than those seen in most churches today, requiring whole boughs, as in this entry from 1457-8 from St. Ewen's in Bristol:

For condels [candles] and bowes ageyne Christesmas...... iiij d.

The accounts for 1468-9 for the same church specify Holly boughs under one of its medieval names derived from 'holm', as in: *For talowe candels and holmyn bowes agaynes Christmesse... iiij d.*

Normally entries are very basic:

For holme and yve [ivy] amenst Cristmas...j d.
St. Mary at Hill, London, 1427-8
Holly and eyvy agenst Crestomas....ij d
St. Helen's, Worcester, 1529
For holly and Ivey at Xmas....iiij d.
St. Peter's Cheap, London 1534
For Holy and Ive against Chrystmas....iiij d
St. Mary Woolnoth, London, 1539
For yve and holye at Chrystemas....ij d.
Ludlow, 1540
Holly at crystmas....j d.
St. Edmund, Salisbury, 1557-8
Payed for hollye bayes and rosemary at Christmas....vj d.
St. Mary-le-Port, Bristol, 1580
Pd for Holly and Ivy, Rosemary and Bayes at Christmass....1 10
St. Laurence, Reading, 1644
Paid for holly ivy and other herbage to White....ij s. vj d.
St. Michael, Bristol, 1644

How the decorations were set up is unknown. No doubt much of the material was distributed around the building in much the same way as today. Certainly whole bunches of Holly were used in parishes like St. Mary Woolnoth because they had to buy string (packthread):

To Goodman Plommer the xxiiijth day of December for to buy holly for the churche and for packthryd to tuy up the same....ix d.   1566-7

Some churches hung the Holly across the church on cords and there are some clues as to the possibility that special structures were made and perhaps hoisted up into an association with the great rood. Through such rituals we begin to see Holly being brought into proximity, physically as well as spiritually, with Christ. Furthermore, just as Hawthorn was set up on one of the Lady Days to represent the Virgin Mary so, it seems, a special Holly structure was sometimes instated to serve as another representation of Christ, called simply the Holyn or Holly, hence:

For holyns to make the holyn of....v d.
St. Mary-on-the-Hill, Chester, 1536-7

Very often there are entries for buying extra candles, often tallow ones, accompanying Holly entries which again suggests Holly was used to make a focal sacred point, made clearer in the 1503 entry from St. Margaret at Westminster: *For candyll for the holy Busche....iiij d.*

That tallow was specified tells us these candles were for general lighting of the feature rather than being involved in Christ's mass itself, since the Catholic Church decreed that all candles for mass services had to be made of nothing but pure beeswax.

Most of the churchwardens' accounts referred to come from urban churches but this should not be taken to indicate that rural parishes did not perform the same rituals. Rather, it's the case that urban records have survived in greater numbers. Additionally, we would expect rural churches to have been given Holly free of charge by local landowners. Maybe people went out gathering it specially, as hinted at by a 1465 record from Thame, in Oxfordshire, where they 'gave' to children a halfpenny to gather Ivy. Beware though, Ivy was classed as a useful weed whereas Holly was a valued resource and so landowners were probably very wary of people just taking it. Maybe the presentation of Holly to the church was another Christmas ritual. There was obviously a good trade in the tree from the country to the towns for the churchwardens to be able to go out and buy what they needed, or could get. The quote above for doing this on 24th December reveals that in some places at least it was deemed inappropriate to deck the church before the Eve of the Feast. That probably applied to homes as well since the notion persists today.

Gradually, it would seem, Holly became symbolic of the body of Christ. That idea was therefore able to survive the Puritan period better than some other rituals that were deemed to be too popish. Nevertheless, come November 19th 1644 Parliament declared that Sunday was the *"only standing holy day under the New Testament"* and within a week they wiped out all others. A new national liturgy was presented to Parliament and this became law on January 4th 1645. It made no provision for Christmas services. Parishes carried on regardless so in 1647 that was made a punishable offence. Parishes still persisted. Particularly defiant was the Church of St. Margaret right beside the Houses of Parliament! They decorated as usual ready for the service, which cost them one shilling and sixpence for Rosemary and Bay – plus three pounds
"Paid in fees unto Mr Friend and Mr Denham, twoe of the messengers unto the serjeant att armes, attending the Common House of Parliament, when their occomptants were committed for permitting ministers to preach upon Christmas day and for adorning the church."

Hascombe
B. wey

Hascombe Church, Surrey, rebuilt by Henry Woodyer in 1864, when he took great trouble, not only with the late 13th century style of architecture but also with the interior decoration. It's one of the best examples of its date in the country and echoes the schemes that would have been fashionable in the Middle Ages when they were supplemented with the Holly and other evergreen decorations.

AFTER CHRISTMAS

As the ritual roles of the Holly roll on from one important day to another there ought to be one that marks the end of its use and of all Christmas celebrations. With Yule having been authorised for twelve days by the Saxons we have, by tradition, declared that the Holly and all other seasonal decorations should be taken down on Twelfth Night. When is that? Twelfth Day is undoubtedly 6th January but is the night that of 5th/6th or of the 6th/7th? The reference books disagree over this but are increasingly falling in line with popular practice and declaring that it is the evening of the 6th. The Holly etc. should be out by midnight and not run into the 7th. Having a set final day was obviously important, since employers didn't want indolent workers extending their Christmas indefinitely! Possibly, for this reason, there are dire superstitious warnings as to what will undoubtedly happen should this be ignored. As far as the Holly is concerned, it will become evil or the harbinger of evil, often personified as elves or other 'little folk' of a malevolent disposition.

"To keep Holly in the house after Twelfth Night
is to invite in the Devil"

What is less clear is what to do with the Holly. Lots of people will tell you to burn it while just as many will throw up their hands in horror and pronounce that to be the worst thing to do. There does not seem to be a 'correct' action to take. To burn it is to return it to the most powerful of elements and thereby reduce it to a spiritual form and that would be in keeping with other ritual practices. Of course there are always exceptions! It doesn't seem any less sacrilegious to dump it, drop it in the dustbin or poke it through the shredder.

"Mother always liked to burn all the bits of holly on Twelfth Night. In fact it was more like she insisted that they, the witches, be burned. To me it seemed as if we were burning all the nasty things that had happened during the year. This was a sort of new beginning, sort of saying sorry for all the bad tempers and things we'd done wrong and making a resolution to be better – a bit like New Year resolutions. This was certainly my interpretation of why we did it. It was quite a solemn affair or seemed so when I was quite young. I still call it 'burning the witches' and always do it on Twelfth Night (evidence submitted in 2000)

Other informants gave assurances that at least one piece of the Holly must be kept in the house throughout the year to hold God's blessing and bring good luck while at the same time warding off evil. That is in keeping with other ritual practices such as keeping the 'Herbs of St. John' from one Midsummer to the next. However, in general, it seems to be accepted in the popular culture that Holly loses its sanctity after Twelfth Night. That's not always been the case. In the 17th century poem about Candlemas, by Robert Herrick of Cornwall, we read that the decorations were not taken down until Candlemas (2nd February):

"Down with the Rosemary, and so
Down with the baies and mistletoe;
Down with the Holly, Ivy all
Wherewith ye drest the Christmas hall."

Rosemary –
another favoured evergreen but one associated more with the Virgin Mary than with Christ.

Other people kept Holly till Shrove Tuesday. One informant in S. E. England still puts some under the pan for the first pancake, just as her mother did in Cheshire, and her mother before that, in the Wirral, where the practice might have arrived by sea from the Isle of Man, where other informants knew the practice. She couldn't remember the reasoning behind this. Quite possibly it is for practical reasons, since the Holly burns so hotly, giving off the extra heat needed for cooking pancakes. Also recorded is the keeping of some Holly till the approach of the next Christmas and then use it to light the fire over which the Christmas pudding is to be cooked. Whatever the origins of these practices they end up being a crucial reassurance that all will be well, since the right thing was done in the right way at the right time. In our times, of insurance policies, freezers full of food, pharmacies, central heating, etc. it is difficult to imagine how fearsome *tomorrow* would once have been.

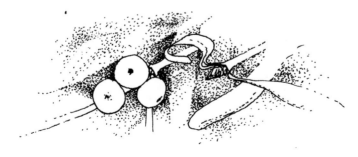

Mistletoe

The Starling is the companion bird to the Holly in the Celtic tree calendar and alphabet. They represent the letter T for the Tinne month, 8th July – 4th August.

THE HOLLY KING

Another strand of the Holly story, entwined through some of the others, is centred upon the allegory that the year was ruled over by two kings who ruled successively in a perpetual cycle. These two kings are represented by the Holly and the Oak. This concept was widespread through the early cultures with Cronos being the Greek equivalent of the Holly King and Saturn, with his Holly club, being the Roman. The concept was known to the Celtic peoples in Britain.

There are varying opinions, conjectures and interpretations about the way the Celtic calendar functioned but there is general agreement that Midsummer and Midwinter were highly significant dates. They were the days for crowning the new king, if, as many believe, they ruled for six months each. The Oak led the year into summer and the Holly then led it on to Midwinter, or, as other interpretations would have it, the Holly King was crowned at Midwinter. As usual there are wonderful allegorical stories to help teach the knowledge to the youngsters of the society. One of the British examples is still well known and appreciated today, as *Sir Gawain and the Green Knight*, from the stories of King Arthur. This surviving version dates from about 1400, although it contains far older material.

22

The earliest surviving version of all is in the Irish tales of Cuchulain, (*Bricreud's Feast*), which dates from 1100 but again it contains far older material.[12] The Welsh version can be found in the story of Rhiannon in the *Mabinogion*. That collection includes the story of *Bran* and the bringing of his head to England. It was buried where the Tower of London now stands and is reputedly guarded by the famous ravens there. Thus it is said that should those ravens leave, then London will fall (because time has been interrupted). Being beheaded is vital to the allegories. The *Green Knight*, arrived at the court of King Arthur, bearing his symbolic bunch of Holly (Holly club in some rewrites):

"Bot in his honde he hade a holyn bobbe,"
But in his hand he had a holly bob/bunch
(Tolkien ed.)

He challenged anyone there to strike off his head. *Sir Gawain* took up the contest and won. Then the *Green Knight* bent over, picked up his head and tucked it under his arm from where the mouth challenged Gawain to a return match in a year's time. Thus the cycle of time continues – summer never wins, winter always returns.

We still sing about this today! It is the basis of the earliest versions of the Christmas carol, *The Holly and the Ivy*, wherein

"Of all the trees that are in the wood,
The holly bears the crown."

The Christian version of this centres upon St. John the Baptist who heralds the coming of Jesus but gets beheaded at Midsummer. John is succeeded by Jesus and thereby arises yet another link between Christ and the Holly. For those who want to explore symbolism even further, the Summer King is a white horse while the Holly King/Christ is the unicorn. Medieval church art showed the unicorn with its head in the lap of a virgin girl which it had found in the forest, representing the incarnation and death of Christ. This image links with high Renaissance art as the *pieta*, or the dead Christ in the lap of the Virgin Mary after the descent from the Cross.

In thee is God become a child,
Ine thee is wreche become mild;
That unicorn that was so wild
Aleyd is of a cheaste;   [allayed by a chaste woman]
Thou hasd itamed and istild......   [tamed and subdued]
with melke of thy breste.

(14th century, English)

---

[12] Irish literature contains the oldest material in Europe north of the Alps.

Returning to *The Holly and Ivy*, this was once a popular ballad, before it became restricted to Christmas. It was sung in taverns as 'rough music' to suspected adulterers! The notion of adultery is an integral part of the old allegories, where honour is all important. In *Sir Gawain and the Green Knight*, it was during Gawain's year's journey to a remote chapel for the return match that he was tempted to adultery and resisted. He did, however, err from true honour in a minor way and so does get his neck cut at the match, but crucially, was not beheaded. In the allegory of the carol, just as Mary stays loyal to Jesus so the woman must cling to her man, otherwise she's out in the cold (isolated from the Church) catching chilblains (kibes). The same affliction (at a time when such was seen as a punishment from God) was wished upon all adulterous men.

Ivy and her gentle women
Sit without in fold,
With a pair of kibed
Heels caught in the cold –
So would I that every man had
That with Ivy will hold.   (15th century)

In general then, and certainly in the popular culture of ballads in the taverns, Ivy never shed its Bacchanalian associations that kept it in ill-repute, whereas Holly became esteemed. Anyone who spoke against it would be hanged!

Who so ever ageinst holly do crie,
In a lepe shall he hang full hie.   [*lepe* rope or basket]
Who so ever agaeinst holly do sing,
He maye wepe and handes wring.   (15th century)

Ultimately, Holly and Ivy, *"now both full grown"* settle peacefully into Christmas carols, but still *"the holly bears the crown."*

FIRE FESTIVALS

The calendar of British festivals contains several exciting fire festivals, mostly in Scotland, at the turn of the year. Although claimed as traditional they are not of an unbroken tradition but revivals. Many more have fallen into history and rarely did any have anything specifically to do with Holly. An exception was once performed in Northern England when a blazing Holly tree was borne through the streets, and teams from local pubs fought for the burning fragments. This has similarities with some of the other fire festivals, such as 'Burning the Clavie,' which is now restricted to Burghead, in Grampian, on 11th January (Old

24

New Year's Eve/Hogmanay). A team member runs in competition through the streets bearing a burning tar barrel (clavie) on his shoulders until it eventually has to be thrown clear. It shatters and sends burning fragments flying. To be hit by one is good luck, while to grab and hold on to one means even better luck and apparently this virtue is still effective if fragments are posted to relatives far away around the world. Pieces are saved to become kindling for next year's clavie.

In these and similar rituals there is always a highly ranked leader, like the King of the Clavie, which seems to echo that ancient idea of the midwinter battle of the kings or gods. However, it is dangerous to think of these as irrefutably linked now that we are so far removed in time from their origins. Such links may not be valid at all.

OTHER FESTIVE DAYS

To my superstitious Welsh mother the Christmas Holly was 'the body of Jesus' and so it was not allowed into the house until Christmas Eve, or rather not until after midnight. Upon enquiry I remember her replying smartly: *"Well! You can't have Jesus arriving before his birthday, can you?"* Mothers know best! Similarly, neither she, nor any other female, dare touch the Holly since to touch the body of Jesus was deemed *'unseemly.'* Consequently father had to stay up late to put up the Holly, under mother's direction of course. Although the association between Holly and Jesus is medieval, to *say* that the tree *is* the body of Jesus is probably far later but documentary evidence has proved elusive.

The obvious place to check this is in the records of the annual celebration of Christ's body Corpus Christi day – when the Church honoured the Eucharist. This annual church celebration arrived late on the scene, being instituted by Pope John XXII in 1317. As much of its purpose was to focus attention on the Real Presence of Christ in the consecrated host it obviously became a prime target at the Reformation. In England, it survived the reforms of Henry VIII but fell foul of the parliament of Edward VI (1547), only to be restored by a royal proclamation of Mary in 1554 and banned again, by Elizabeth in 1559.

There was resistance to its abolition since it had become far more than a church service. The candle-lit processions had gone out into the streets, where, as a public holiday, they had become an important social event in the calendar. They provided some of the year's best entertainment because apart from the lavish processions there were soon extensive drama cycles. These were often adopted and paid for by the trade guilds and became crucially significant in the history of the development of English stage drama. Even when the church service was banned many communities wanted to persist with their annual drama festival. Usually they had the tact (or guile) to edit out material likely to offend the new Protestant officialdom. Scotland held out longest.

Corpus Christi took place in late spring or early summer, depending when Easter fell, for Corpus Christi was the second Thursday after Whitsun. It was therefore ideally placed for floral decorations and records show they were much used. If Holly was considered in those times to represent the Body of Christ then surely this was its day. However, the Churchwarden accounts for expenditure on the decorations do not draw attention to Holly as they do at Christmas. Instead, Roses and Woodruff were the preferred flowers dedicated to this festival. Getting them both in bloom on this day would have been difficult, if not impossible, in those years when Easter was early.

Holly cannot be ruled out altogether as there are entries in some accounts for greenery, without specifying the plants. However, the expenditure was to buy materials for making up garlands to be worn, for which prickly Holly would not have been well suited. They were to be worn by the priests and apparently by other significant figures in the processions. Perhaps some were given as a tactful gesture to local benefactors present, such as when St. Mary-at-Hill spent three pence in 1520 on a garland each for *"Mr Doctor and the parish prest"*.

26

Using Holly in garlands doesn't sound very comfortable! At least the roses could be trimmed. That noted, it should also be said that very little *detailed* information survives about this day; even descriptions and scripts of the all important drama cycles leave many a question unanswered. With the garlands it is possible that if Holly was used at all it was reserved for garlanding static sites, such as three crosses at St. Mary-at-Hill in the same entry as above. Indeed, these garlands were often listed separately, as in 1491 when the same church *"Paid at Corpus Cristi tyde for garnyssyng of xij torches at iijd the pece"* (three shillings) and then 13 pence *"Pd for rose garlandes"*. All in all, the church paid for 65 garlands for that one day in 1520. It was obviously a grand procession and presumably many parishioners arrived bedecked in their own garlands.

Apart from Corpus Christi Day it's not very clear to us today where else in the records evidence should be sought. Easter would be another prime contender and indeed there are Holly memories for that time but the usage seems to have been rare. John Evelyn reminded the Royal Society in 1662 that *"we still dress up both our Churches and Houses, on Christmas and other Festival* Days" with Holly. Sadly, he doesn't go on to list those other festive days.

TIME FOR REVIVAL

Henry VIII is remembered as a king who really knew how to have a lavish time. When he was newly crowned there was plenty of opportunity with the calendar packed with ritual celebrations, most of which had church connections. Henry's break with Rome did little to curtail this. It was the government of his succeeding son, Edward VI, that implemented Protestant reforms on a massive and lasting scale. For a short time there were returns to the old ways under Catholic Mary, but these were reversed again by Henry's other daughter, the Protestant Elizabeth I. Thus by the end of her reign Elizabeth had a realm that was almost barren of the wealth of ritual celebrations that had been so enjoyed by her father as a young man. A period of even greater austerity was to follow, under the reforming zeal of the Puritans leading to the Civil Wars. With the Restoration of Charles II Christmas was reinstated but it was now rather isolated after the abolition of so much. There was no great festival for twelve days.

With the flourishing of antiquarian interests during the 18th century all sorts of old midwinter and Christmas ideas resurfaced so that by 1800 Christmas was being well and truly celebrated again. This was primarily a domestic family affair rather than the overspilling of a church festival. There were foreign imports too. Americans had been over to collect Old World traditions for a new sales gimmick which they sent over as Father Christmas, while from Germany came the Christmas tree. By 1840 all the elements of a modern Christmas were in place. These were of course for the middle classes, which had expanded dramatically with newly enriched merchants and industrialists through the Industrial Revolution. The impoverished working classes, without money or holidays, had a very meagre Christmas but they still had one. Going carol singing became a popular way of getting a few extra pennies for the occasion. Around Exmoor the carollers were called 'Holly Riders' since they wore sprigs of Holly on their coats and all around their hats. In return for their singing they were given cakes and cider and, if they were lucky, pennies.[13]

Then our top writer produced a piece of fiction that caused a social revolution – one of the very few pieces of fiction in the world to achieve this. It was Charles Dickens with his *Christmas Carol*. It had the effrontery to suggest that the working classes should have the same rights to celebrate Christmas as their employers. It was well targeted since only the employers were literate enough to read the story! Being released in serial form gave the message time to be absorbed. Not being a single volume at that stage saved it from being burnt as heresy on a social bonfire. Inflamed employers found that a good story travels fast and steadily the Christmas holiday was offered widely.

Nevertheless, it took a hundred years – until after the Second World War – to become the norm. In the late 1940s estate workers, in some places, were still expected to work over Christmas Day and Boxing Day, albeit for shorter hours. One informant related starting work for British Rail in 1947 and found that when it came to signing the contract she had to decide which Bank Holiday she wanted – an English Christmas Day or a Scottish New Year's Day/Hogmanay – since the railway lines crossed the borders! She couldn't have both and she couldn't change her mind. Christmas Day was not granted as a Bank Holiday in Scotland until 1958.

VICTORIAN AND EDWARDIAN DECORATIONS

Through all this period the Holly had remained the prime decorative evergreen. This was primarily because it could often be got free by country people. They also raised extra pennies selling it on to the townsfolk as recalled by George Rutter in *A Country Lad at Heart*. As Gloucestershire schoolboys early in the 20th century they would meet up with the farmer on a Saturday morning to go off along the hedgerows to send an agile lad up the standard trees to saw off well-berried branches. Hollies were always left as standards, he

---

[13] see Hutton, p.61

remembered, since they would knock the witches off their broomsticks when they flew along the lines of the hedges. The other boys tried to break the fall of the boughs so as not to dislodge too many berries. Then it was all carted back to a barn to be cut into saleable lengths ready to go to market. The boys got a shilling and a pocketful of apples.

Small, well-formed trees, had a market too, as Christmas trees for those who couldn't afford a conifer. The first dated reference to the conifer Christmas tree in England is 1800 and by the 1840s it was becoming very popular but the newspapers and magazines of the time were still having to inform their readers of its meaning and the manner in which it should be decorated. The Holly versions were small, not just because of the cost or because workers' cottages were cramped but because they were a windowsill decoration. When fully decorated they were put in the lighted window, without the curtains being drawn, for the admiration of passers-by outside. Local houses would compete for the most admired tree.

Holly, as a Christmas tree, persisted until after the Second World War. Then, landowners who had extended their ploughland for the war effort wanted to keep it productive. They needed a quick maturing cash crop that was not labour intensive and so thousands of acres of Christmas tree plantations became part of the rural scene. The conifers could be sold cheaply as the 'correct' thing to have and the Holly trees fell from favour.

Being 'correct' or more precisely, being 'tasteful', had become a major concern. Through late Victorian and Edwardian times the press, particularly ladies' magazines, went to great lengths in their articles to ensure their readers would know how to decorate for Christmas *tastefully*. Obviously the emphasis is on the middle classes and some of the directions would require such large amounts of material that it is hardly surprising that the provision of mixed evergreens of all sorts became such big business for the rural areas supplying towns and big houses. Holly was paramount, since it was sanctioned by the Church and wouldn't upset the Establishment whereas Mistletoe, which hadn't been Christianised, could well cause offence. There could also be problems with pagan/Catholic Ivy. Nevertheless, if it were green somebody would buy it, including moss.

Middle class decorative schemes were lavish. Some articles required the reader to cover the whole ceiling, so skill and ingenuity were required. Covering whole walls would have been slightly easier. Then the windows and door frames, mirrors and pictures all had to be framed with Holly and its seasonal associates – including heads of coloured everlasting flowers, cotton wool, tinfoil, and moss. Coloured everlasting flowers were very popular because with those it was possible and popular to spell out a seasonal message as part of enormous wall designs. Even 'Happy Christmas' required dozens of flower heads and many more for 'A Hundred Thousand Welcomes' while verses from the Bible could really show off the household's wealth.

Finally, and seemingly most daunting of all, was the great central feature for the Christmas dining table. A long mirror could be the starting point as a 'lake' around which a miniature landscape could be created. Whatever the design, it should be so low as not to obstruct your view of the diners opposite. Only in the very grandest of houses were the tables so large that there was room to overcome this problem. Then the Holly etc. might find itself elevated on pedestals above the line of sight and conversation.

All this was ostensibly for the children, with the decorating providing a welcome relief from the limited and therefore repetitive range of pastimes. Indeed, the whole of this Christmas revival was directed towards the children. That said, the end result of the decorations shouldn't look childish. It had to impress the adult guests with its finesse and good taste. The press articles from the time shovel scorn and derision on anyone satisfied with just a vase of Holly on the table!

THE GREEN HOLLY RITUAL

The *green* holly ritual of my childhood seems to have died out. *Green* Holly meant unberried Holly. It was given by employers to their estate workers as a gesture of appreciation of their year's work and therefore an indication that contracts would be renewed next Lady Day. I well remember the year, in the late 1950s, when my father didn't get his! There was considerable consternation as this foretold eviction and there was much debate as to what offence he'd caused. Then the boss arrived late on Christmas Eve, bearing a large armful, plus profuse apologies and excuses. Apparently this practice was extended also to retired workers who were well remembered, judging from a recollection recorded by Gertrude Jekyll in her *Old West Surrey*, published in 1904: *"Best place I ever lived in was at Mr. Woods's at Hambledon. Quietest and best master I ever lived with...After I left, there was always a bit of green holly at Christmas..."* So far I haven't traced a reference to this from an urban setting, just in the countryside.

THE MAGICAL TREE

In 1893 The Lady magazine reported, *"...our West Country girls have a pretty custom of trimming their beds with holly on Christmas Eve. They say the evil spirits will harm them if they omit this Christmas custom."* Many hundreds of other such statements abounded at this time during an enthusiasm for traditional lore. Much of it was nothing of the sort. Many practices cannot be traced back very far and so we don't know whether they are indeed of ancient origin or modern invention. Some certainly echo ancient ideas, such as the notion that certain plants held the knowledge of our future love lives, which they could be persuaded to reveal. Holly was one such plant of divination. Thus girls should put Holly leaves under the pillow in order to see their future husband in their dreams. Apparently this doesn't work very well and neither does the notion that carrying a bag of Holly berries and leaves makes a young man more attractive to girls. A more elaborate ritual is said to ensure fulfilment of any dream but as this has to be done before going to sleep the person must have supreme confidence in the nature of their dreams. Anyway, what you do is this: in complete silence, gather nine Holly leaves on a Friday night after midnight and tie them with nine knots into a white cloth which must then be secreted under the pillow. Dream on!

There was a boys' version too and in some rituals the two types of foliage were used accordingly, since the prickly leaves were considered 'male' and leaves without prickles were 'female'. If the female foliage was used as Christmas decoration it informed everyone that the woman ruled the house. Such female foliage is comparatively scarce so the male leaves were the norm just as it was for the man to rule his household. To prevent the woman having any option in the matter the man ensured the Holly was brought into the house ahead of the Ivy. Obviously this worked very well, for when the Victorians included Holly in their 'Language of Flowers' it was to symbolise domestic harmony!

In terms of domestic harmony, Holly was often believed to be the domain of the 'Little People' and to break bits off brought retaliation. Readers will find constant contradictions in the lore. That is normal. It depends where you live and at what period. In parts of Ireland it is taboo not only to cut a Holly, as the fairies' abode, but to grow it anywhere near the house for fear of it attracting unwelcome Little People. Hence they call it the Gentle Tree. In England, on the other hand, it was popularly grown beside the house to ward off witches. The timber has been used for the making of thresholds so that the protective powers would dissuade Little Outsiders from entering the house, while indoors, it warded off house goblins or brownies, sometimes called Robin Goodfellow or Hobthrust. Brownies are invaluable assets to any home but they must not be crossed. These beliefs affect the tree's practical uses. For example, bunches of Holly have been used as chimney brushes in England but not in Ireland as that would break both the above taboos. Some people, however, deliberately chose Holly in the belief that a chimney cleaned with Holly would never catch fire.

Folklore says lightning never strikes a Holly, which may be well founded. They like to grow under taller Oaks and are therefore less likely to be struck, while the lore that says Oaks attract lightning does seem to have truth in it. Thus the Oak was the sacred tree of thunder gods, such as Thor and Zeus. To bring Holly into the house would afford protection from storms and fire. Tramps spent the night under Hollies, for their protection, and if they found a good one they returned to it time and again. Such specimens often got local names as 'Tramp Tree'. Apart from safeguarding themselves from evil spirits, tramps knew it was the driest and most sheltered place. Holly boughs droop towards the ground as they mature, to form a full skirt of foliage to deter nosy intruders, to keep out the wind, and to shield against rain. The dense shade around the trunk suppresses all vegetation (even brambles!) so there's no problem about setting up a sleeping place.

A crucial factor is the red berries. Red was considered the colour of the gods and so red items were protective:

Rowan trees and red thread
Hold all evil in their dread.

Like the Rowan, the Holly was protective against all evil spirits, demons and the Evil Eye. The Irish wouldn't agree and their tradition of it being an unlucky

Rowan berries

tree goes right back to the early cultures of the Mediterranean, recorded in the writings of Macrobius etc. That said, Irish traditions that it is unlucky to cut the Holly may date from old Irish laws that made this illegal because it was one of their ancient sacred trees.[14]

Turning to Christian lore, we find there is rather a lot of it! Much of it tests our credulity. Of course these may not represent the formal teachings of the Church but derive from *aide memoires* used in the teaching of Bible stories, whether at home or in Sunday Schools and Church Schools from the second half of the 19th century. Any earlier material may have its roots in the drama cycles

---

[14] one of the Seven Chieftain Trees but not all that is written about those is well-founded.

performed from the late Middle Ages onwards, but not enough of the scripts survive to know with any certainty. The following are the six examples sent in most frequently by informants in 1999:-

Holly grows only in the footprints of Jesus.

Holly wood was used for the Cross and thereafter the Holly grew prickly leaves to remind us of the Crown of Thorns.

The white blossom represents the purity of Christ's Ministry.

The red berries represent beads of blood on Christ's forehead beneath the Crown of Thorns. Before the Crucifixion all Holly berries were said to be yellow.

Berries first appeared after a lamb had been caught in a Holly bush on the way to the Nativity.

Robins got their red breasts while pecking the berries from the Crown of Thorns made from Holly.

Finally, a note on the touchy subject of weather forecasting. In common with other berry-bearing trees and shrubs, it is often said that when the Holly bears a heavy crop of berries it foretells a hard winter. It doesn't. It reflects the previous summer's weather when it was dry and sunny enough to ripen the new wood ready for bearing flowers next year. Good pollination is obviously essential and so a heavy crop of berries also reflects good weather during flowering time, showing the pollinating insects, including the honey bee, were active. The temperature is critical too; the July average needs to be at least 12°C.[15]

---

[15] according to Beckett, p.33, but not widely published

Whether it's a hard winter or not, Holly berries are very attractive to birds such as Waxwings and members of the thrush family such as Song Thrushes, Mistle Thrushes, Blackbirds, Fieldfares and Redwings (illus). In severe weather other birds feed on them too.

THE PRACTICAL USES

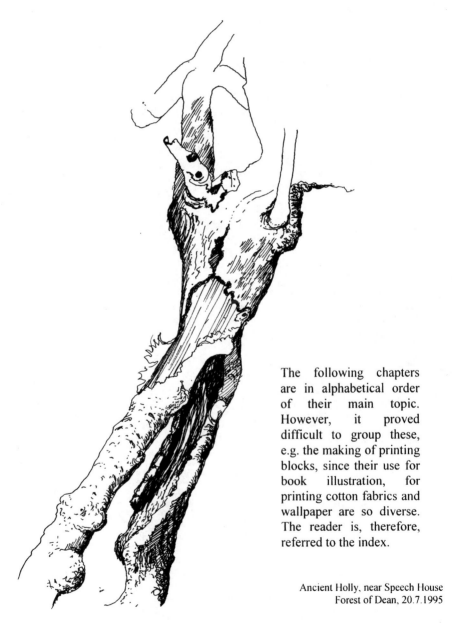

The following chapters are in alphabetical order of their main topic. However, it proved difficult to group these, e.g. the making of printing blocks, since their use for book illustration, for printing cotton fabrics and wallpaper are so diverse. The reader is, therefore, referred to the index.

Ancient Holly, near Speech House
Forest of Dean, 20.7.1995

BIRDLIME AND THE BIRD CATCHER

Although the rat-catcher and the gamekeeper are well known, those who trapped rodents and little birds receive scant attention in our social history books. Small birds were trapped regularly, for sale, for food and as part of pest control. Among the strategies employed was the use of 'birdlime', a viscous glue of plant origin. Indeed, the word *viscous* comes from the Greek word *viskos* meaning "thick with leaves" or "full of birdlime". Hence the Latin *viscum* for birdlime. This word was taken to name the genus *Viscum* for the Mistletoe, because of the very sticky sap in the berries that became a prime raw material for birdlime. However, Mistletoe berries are obviously seasonal and not available in large quantities. A source to overcome those problems was found in the bark of the Holly. That is explained in more detail below but first, some extra details to set the scene.

Pest control has always been necessary so it is hardly surprising to find references to birdlime in the Classical writings from Greece. Today, farmers have problems with flocks of Canada Geese and migratory Swan species but in the past it was the small birds that could be a major problem. Flocks of finches descended into the flax fields to strip the linseed and so got the name Linnet. The rickyards and threshing floors attracted different finches to forage among the chaff for broken grains and these became known as Chaffinches. Gluey birdlime was spread on nearby perches, or else such perches were provided, so that when the birds alighted and got their feet trapped the bird-catcher could run out and snatch them off.

Chaffinch – among the prime targets for pest control and also one that could be sold on as a songbird for caging, especially the more colourful males.

These birds were eaten. *Four and twenty blackbirds baked in a pie* is not just a nursery rhyme. Birds ranging from Skylarks to Blackbirds could be bought in the markets, from say the 16th –19th centuries, for about 2d a dozen and can still be bought in pies on the Continent today. Real Blackbirds were soon replaced by a sort of meatball but baked pies were not the food of the average labourer. His food came out of the cooking pot as a stew or *mess* so we still say a muddle of things is a mess. The older meaning is echoed in the armed forces with soldiers' mess tins and the officers' mess etc. or in hospitals with a surgeons' mess. When birds and other 'rubbish' meat were added then the mess became a *trash*, preserved in America as their word for rubbish. Thus the little birds were part of the labourers' protein diet but could also be bartered or sold. Our ancestors wasted nothing.

Male Blackbird

Songbirds could be sold alive as cage-birds. These were not only hung up in the home but in the streets as well, as in Birdcage Walk in London. Many a 19th century romantic painting of rural cottages shows the birdcage hanging outside the door in the sun for the day. Of course many of these birds must have pined for their freedom and died, so keeping up a steady demand from the bird-catchers. In the early 1900s this was still perfectly acceptable and so an issue of the *Boys Own Book of Outdoor Sports* of the time includes an article on 'Bird Trapping: tips and technique'.

This trade persisted in Britain until the 1930s. Then, the respected countryman and writer, Eric Parker, as editor of *The Field*, initiated a campaign through that publication to draw the public's attention to the cruelty involved. Prospective customers had not been aware that the little birds singing so heartily were in fact suffering the pain of being secretly stabbed in the eye with a needle by the street-trader. This was such big business that Eric Parker and his journalists received death threats and needed police protection. At the same time, Parker's wife and daughter Mary, took up the cause through the Surrey branch of the Federation of Women's Institutes, all the way to the Annual General Meeting in the Royal Albert Hall. Due to the backing from this large and powerful lobby Britain soon had the 1935 *Wild Birds Protection Act*. Further legislation has followed. All the same, in the year 2000 birdlime is still being used, illegally, to trap wild birds for the cagebird market. It is worth the risk of being caught, apparently, since the birds fetch about £40 a pair while the fines from a successful prosecution are being levied at just a few hundred pounds, instead of anything near the maximum fine of £1,000 per bird, plus £5,000 depending on the trapping method.[1]

As for rodents, these too were trapped with birdlime. It is said that the earliest European reference to trapping birds and rodents is a figure in the *Olaus Magnus* of 1555 but note the quotation below from Machiavelli of 1513. In the early 18th century was published *The Compleat Vermin-Killer* which says, for taking for rats and mice:

"Take a Board three foot square, and lay a piece of rusty fry'd Bacon in the middle, then lay it pretty thick with Birdlime, leaving some Alleys for 'em to come to it, and they'l get among the Birdlime and stick, drawing and squeaking, that it will make you Sport. One said he has catch'd 12 in a Night. In Staffordshire they put Birdlime about their holes, and they running among it, it sticks to their Skins, that they will not leave scratching till they kill themselves."

Staying with mammals for a moment, rods of Holly 3 feet 6 inches to 4 feet long and as thick as a finger were used on the Continent in the spring-traps for catching Dormice alive. Exact measurements and directions for the construction of these traps are given in chapter XXXI of *Les Ruses Innocentes* for hunting and fishing. Written in French,[2] it was published in Amsterdam in 1695. This may well refer to the much larger Edible Dormouse,[3] which was a Continental delicacy, especially in Italy, and remains so today. It was not a British native but Lord Rothschild introduced some in 1902.[4]

The recipes for making birdlime are so readily available that there seems little point withholding from them here but the following recipe is for education only. To *use* birdlime is illegal. These are John Evelyn's directions (17thC):-

"Peel a good Quantity of the Bark about Midsummer; fill a Vessel with it, and put to it Spring-water: then boil it, till the gray and white Bark rise from the green, which will require near twelve Hours boiling; then taking it off the Fire, separate

---

[1] National Farmers' Union website November 2000.
[2] with thanks to Liz. Willis for the translation
[3] known also as the Fat, Grey or Squirrel-tailed Dormouse, *Glis glis.*
[4] so now found wild in the Chilterns, in the triangle between Aylesbury, Beaconsfield and Luton.

the Barks, the Water first well drained from it: Then lay the green Bark on the Earth, in some cool Vault or Cellar, covering it with any Sort of green and rank Weeds, such as Dock, Thistles, Hemlock, etc. to a good Thickness: Thus let it continue near a Fortnight, by which Time 'twill become a perfect Mucilage: Then pound it all exceedingly in a Stone Mortar, till it be a tough Paste, and so very fine, as no Part of the Bark be discernable: This done, wash it accurately well in some running Stream of Water, as long as you perceive the least Ordure or Motes in it, and so reserve it in some earthen Pot, to purge and ferment, scumming it as often as anything arises for four or five Days, and when no more Filth comes, change it into a fresh Vessel of Earth, and reserve it for Use, thus: Take what Quantity you please of it and in an earthen Pipkin, add a third Part of Capons or Goose-grease to it, well clarified, or Oil of Walnuts, which is better; incorporate these on a gentle Fire, continually stirring it till it be cold, and thus your Composition is finished."

He doesn't tell us about storage and use though. That can be found in *The Compleat Vermin Killer*[5] wherein we are instructed to *"shift into another Clean Vessel and keep it for your use. When you use it, Put a third Part of Hogs grease, Goose grease or any thin Grease into it, and stir it over a gentle Fire, in an earthen Vessel, till well Incorporated, then take it off and continue stirring until it become cold."*

A shorter but essentially similar version was issued by William Coles in his *Adam in Eden*, of 1657. Although Evelyn specifies Midsummer, birdlime can be manufactured at other times. Certainly it was purchased at other seasons and the fact that this was a marketed product implies that its manufacture was part of it some countrymen's livelihood. For example, the Account Roll of the Manors of Miaxter Priory, 1425, includes in the list of necessary provisions the purchase of 1lb of birdlime for 3d (the same accounts show, for comparison, that this was equal to three days' wages paid "to a certain stranger hired to drive the plough and harrow".)[6]

Among those who used birdlime was none other than the infamous Machiavelli:

"I am living on my farm, and since I had my last bad luck, I have not spent twenty days, putting them all together, in Florence. I have until now been snaring thrushes with my own hands. I got up before day, prepared birdlime, went out with a bundle of cages on my back, so that I looked like Geta when he was returning from the harbor with Amphitryon's books. I caught at least two thrushes and at

---

[5] transcript provided kindly by Mr. David Drummond
[6] R.B.Morgan,ed. Readings in English Social History; CUP, 1923)

most six. And so I did all September. Then this pastime, pitiful and strange as it is, gave out, to my displeasure. And of what sort my life is, I shall tell you.[7]

These Old World practices were taken by colonists to the New World where, it is said, the native peoples did not have knowledge of birdlime yet it is said also that the Iroquois[8] people made it from Slippery Elm (Ulmus rubra). Most people round the world seem to have discovered a plant that has the right properties; it is not specific to Holly and Mistletoe. In America native species of Holly have to be used, so it was probably the American Holly (Ilex opaca) or even the Yaupon (Ilex vomitoria) that Thomas Harriot recorded (1588) in his Briefe and True Report wherein he lists "Holly, a necessary thing for the making of birdlime" under the heading of "Svch other thinges as is be hooful [useful]." There was certainly a demand for birdlime from the colonists. At Williamsburg, in 1774, the apothecary shop advertised new supplies of a wide range of products including birdlime.

Birdlime has also contributed to our literary heritage, in figures of speech concerning tenacious glue. To be effective, figures of speech need to be understood readily and the frequency of birdlime references in all manner of documents, gives a succinct insight into the prevalence of the use of this substance. These are not just literary references for literate readers of Charles Dickens, for example, but they also occur in popular entertainment, such as the plays of Shakespeare, and in workday language such as medieval court records, where prosecuting officers claimed that other people's property stuck to the defendant's fingers like birdlime. Similes are the commonest figure of speech using birdlime. An early metaphorical reference can be found in the *Confessions* of St. Augustine of Hippo, (354-430), wherein he recalled,

"Therefore I fell among men [Manichaeans] proudly raving, very carnal, and voluble, in whose mouths were the snares of the devil—the birdlime being composed of a mixture of the syllables of Thy name, and of our Lord Jesus Christ, and of the Paraclete, the Holy Ghost, the Comforter. These names departed not out of their mouths, but so far forth as the sound only and the clatter of the tongue, for the heart was empty of truth."[9]

Finally, there is the occasional 'tall story' (assuming the truth of the following is open to doubt!):-
"There was a man in the days of our boyhood who lived near Ripley [Surrey], our home in that far-off time, who prided himself greatly on his bird-lime. He told us how he one day spread some liberally along the top shoots of his garden hedge, and, hearing a tremendous twittering, presently went to see how he had fared. The

---

[7] Letter from Niccolo Machiavelli, to Francesco Vettori, 10 December 1513; Florence
[8] when contacted with this question the Iroquois Museum replied, "We have no answer for you."
[9] St. Augustine of Hippo; *Confessions*; Book III, Ch.VI, 10.

birds, hopelessly entangled, made a supreme effort at escape when he appeared, the result being that his hedge was uprooted, and the last he saw of it was its being carried off by the birds out in the direction of Woking. Assuming this story to be true it speaks volumes for the strength of his bird-lime." [10]

BALLOONS AND BIRDLIME

In August 1783 the Montgolfier brothers flew their first hot air balloon over Paris to be followed in ten days by the hydrogen balloon of Jacques Charles. The military implications of these ventures led rapidly to the establishing of the Aerostat Commission, intent upon deciding which of the two technologies was the superior and to devise lighter, less permeable coverings for balloons. Among the scientists involved was Antoine-Laurent de Lavoisier who, working with Berthollet, proposed a double thickness of silk, stretched tightly, and coated with varnish. The varnish had to be flexible, which was a problem, but Lavousier reported:

"Birdlime used for catching birds has been successfully tested; this substance dissolves with effervescence in linseed oil, and the result is an excellent varnish, as flexible as elastic gum." [11]

[10] Hulme; 1902, p.161
[11] Lavoisier, *Correspondence*; Part IV, p.10

THE FARMER AND HORSEMAN

Farmers tend to use up waste wood for fencing posts and hedging stakes but they would turn their backs upon Holly. When driven into moist soil and exposed to the weather Holly deteriorates rapidly.

Keeping pigs was commonplace. Keeping pigs in the right place was a nightmare. They can be both determined and forceful and break out of compounds. Judging from the penalties listed in the earliest Welsh laws, pigs had an enthusiasm for entering farmhouses to wallow in the warm ashes of the fire and thereby spread burning chips into the strewing rushes and set everything alight. Ultimately pig-control incorporated a metal ring through the snout that caused pain when the pig tried rooting its way to freedom. Before that a **skewer** of hard Holly was driven through the snout:-

"*In these Parts* [Newdigate, Surrey] *the Inhabitants do not Yoke their Pigs, to hinder them from breaking Hedges; but thrust Skewers through their Nostrills, which answers the same End, and is not intended with the ill Consequences of hindering their Rest and by that, their Thriving, These skewers are about two or three Inches long, and, thrust through their tender Noses, hinder their breaking through Fences, and rooting up the Earth or any Plants.*"[12]

The prime demand for the wood was for making the heads of **flails** for the threshing of corn. This is a prehistoric technique and one still used in many parts of the world today. In Britain, flailing started to go into decline subsequent to the invention of the mechanical threshing machine by Andrew Meikle in 1784. Nevertheless, the flail persisted in use till the first half of the 20th century. There are memories of its revived use in the 1940s, reflecting necessity, when the Second World War created fuel shortages.

The flail that was used against the corn on the threshing floor is, in simple terms, two straight rods coupled together loosely. Descriptions from the end of their period say each

---

[12] Aubrey, Vol. IV, p. 268

piece was about an ell long - a measurement that became standardised eventually to 45 inches in England and 37.2 inches in Scotland. Early illustrations often show the head or *swingel* shorter than the handle. This was the piece made of very hard wood, such as Holly, Apple, Blackthorn, Hawthorn or Hornbeam.

In use its purpose was to dislodge the grains from the ears but not to split the grain or crush it into the wooden threshing floor. At first this may seem a very minor use of the Holly but when it is remembered that all of a manor's corn had to be treated in this way, whether intended for malting or for flour, such hard timbers take on a greater significance. The daily loaf and a safe drink were absolute essentials for the survival of the community.[13]

When it came to making butter, Holly was used for both butter **pats** and **prints**. The pats are also known as Scotch hands or handles and are the tools like little cricket bats used to pat the freshly churned butter into a more solid mass and then to shape it up into portions. In choosing the wood for these tools our ancestors looked for something strong that would not snap at the shoulders, something without coarse grain to which the butter would adhere and so Beech became a popular choice. Rated more highly was something pale that would show up dirt, which brought Box and Holly into use. These two close-grained woods resisted the effects of moisture that might otherwise lift fibres to either leave little splinters in the butter or make it stick. Our ancestors also realised they could make the task less hard work by shaping a slight taper into the butter pat, like a wedge, from handle to front. Those without this refinement make the wrists ache and are usually modern. *(Illus. left from Dairymaids Flora)*

Having made the butter, the portions were then stamped with a personal design that would act as a trademark in the market

---

[13] further inf. in *Searching for Hornbeam*

44

place. These designs were carved into thick wooden disks, which usually had a handle attached to the back. When the disks or 'prints' were made from Holly it was for the same reasons as for the pats. Alternative woods were Apple, Box and Sycamore. The carved designs were often geometric but there were also motifs from farming life: the cow, orchard blossom, Forget-me-nots from the garden, Roses from the hedgerow, and Thistle heads because the coloured floral parts were a popular rennet for cheese-making. Many of these designs are intricate and beautiful – a fine testimony to the skill and aesthetic sensitivity of country craftsmen. (Illus. below from *Dairymaids Flora*)

Butter Prints

Farmers, battling against adversity in their grim determination to win a return from their land, have always had a rich store of lore to ensure success. Holly was endowed with **supernatural powers.** It was Pliny the Elder, back in the first century, who recorded popular beliefs that the Holly had the power to overcome evil forces afflicting the temperament of animals. These beliefs travelled to Britain and have become embodied in our own lore and either been modified or supplemented. Sprays of Holly were hung up in cowsheds, within living memory, to ensure the well being of the livestock. When they were kept in compounds on cold winter nights, so it was said, a ring of Holly around the outside protected both man and beast from wolves. This may have derived from the practical notion that such a barrier would be highly inflammable and could be ignited at the onset of a wolf-pack attack. Should cattle stampede or horses bolt, the tactic was to throw Holly after them. They would calm and return, even if the Holly fell short. Is this one reason why countrymen were very fond of carrying a Holly walking stick with them? To keep ploughing horses straight in the furrow the ploughman carried a Holly **whipstock**. Outside the agricultural scene the picture was the same, from **riding stocks** to **light driving whips**. To prevent horses bolting or even from becoming disturbed by malevolent forces, they were given **collars** to wear, made of entwined Holly and Bittersweet (*Solanum dulcamara*).

This is basically *sympathetic magic*, with the powers of one thing affecting another. Why the Holly should be regarded as so powerful does not seem to have been recorded by any early writer. It probably derives from Holly having been selected as the symbol for the most powerful forces, like Apollo the sun god. In due course this was adopted by the Christians to symbolise Christ and that ensured it stayed acceptable until the present time. This probably seems very remote in the minds of readers today but would once have been a significant attitude of our rural ancestors. Certainly it was strong enough to penetrate the increasingly industrial landscape when **horsewhips**, **(whipstocks)** had to be mass-produced. The contributors to Mabey's *Flora Britannica* submitted information to the effect that when horse-drawn vehicles were at their peak, 210,000 whips a year were being made. How many Holly trees were being felled each year to sustain that one demand alone? The production of these lasted well into the 20th century for Edlin[14] recorded Holly was "*still in demand by a Birmingham whip factory for whip stocks; for this purpose it needs careful seasoning*". Countrymen made their own, of course, and for long ones needed by carters and ploughmen they took not the trunk or branches but the long straight suckers that can arise around the trunk of a Holly. In areas where it was taboo to *cut* Holly the suckers were 'pulled' from the trunk.[15] All these can still be found in use today and also **walking sticks**. These were made from either the suckers or by a layering technique. For that a young Holly was heeled over and pegged down to the soil surface. New shoots would rise vertically so that in due course the whole sapling was cut and sectioned so that each shoot was cut free with a section of the main stem. The two were more of less at right angles to each other, enabling that piece of main stem to be fashioned into the handle of the stick. In good Holly growing areas, like West Surrey, there were several walking stick factories and these, like the one at Mid Holmwood,[16] included Holly in their range of sticks of course. Evelyn stated that Surrey's Holmwood took its name from the abundance of Holly thereabouts and this has been repeated by writers ever since. It is not correct. The name predates

---

[14] Edlin, p.118
[15] having tried this, I think 'yanked' would have been a more descriptive verb!
[16] with thanks to Muriel Woolven for drawing this site to my attention.

46

the rise of holm as a common name for Holly and in those earlier documents the area is designated Homewood – the wood reserved for the home farm or manorial centre.

When it came to sewing up sacks of grain etc. **wooden needles** were used, when metal ones were not available. This persisted longest in the specialised craft of the fishing-net maker, which Edlin[17] was still able to record from Sussex in the first half of the 20th century.

Turning from the wood to the foliage, Holly has been important as animal **fodder**. This may sound unlikely, bearing in mind the spines on the leaves, but it is believed that the tree evolved those to safeguard itself from browsers, which is why the uppermost foliage, out of an animal's reach, can be devoid of spines. As one of Britain's few sources of green food during the winter it was obviously very attractive to herbivores and man, noticing this, turned to the Holly for winter fodder for all types of livestock, whether, horses, cattle, sheep, deer, goats or even pigs. No doubt this is a very ancient use but the oldest records are from the 13th century. This is to be expected since relatively few records have survived from before this date.

In the 1290s, for example, in West Derbyshire, they were paying two shillings per anum for the right to take Holly as fodder.[18] In other words, in some manors it was not considered part of the usual rights to take it. Stockmen had to pay extra. Thus in 1296/7 there are surviving indictments for removing Holly for fodder from Nidderdale in Yorkshire.[19] Records then continue through to the 18th century, when people were still paying Holly rents but soon Holly begins to feature for a different reason. It was being removed, grubbed out, to make way for more of the sheep pastures that were changing the face of the British Isles.

---

[17] Edlin p.118
[18] see Spray, Martin, which has been the main source for this topic. See also Radley.
[19] Spray

The use of Holly for fodder does not seem to have been universal at any time. It was turned to in times of need and even then only in districts where the soil gave rise to an abundance of the tree. Extra reserves had to be planted specially for the purpose in some places. Cold, exposed districts, especially at higher altitudes, did not suit the Holly either; since late spring frosts retarded the growth, if the Holly would grow at all. Of course these same places, cold and on poor soils, were the very ones that would have benefited from more Holly since they give rise to poor pasture with little to eat in the winter. In terms of sheep, keeping them alive through any winter was vital, since it was their wool, not their meat, which was so important to the national economy. Stock reared for meat could be culled during periods of extreme shortages.

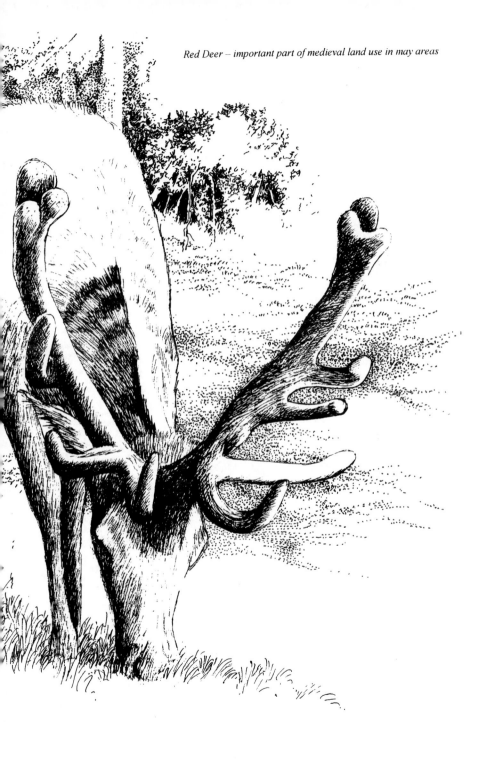

Red Deer – important part of medieval land use in may areas

Cutting Holly fodder was still an important practice in the Lake District in the 1770s but after that it declines sharply until today when some farmers know it can be so used but the majority are unaware. This decline was due largely to changes in agriculture that now meant there were alternative winter feeds. Before the 17th century, stockbreeders had to rely solely upon hay for winter feed but agricultural pioneers, such as Sir Richard Weston of Guildford, Surrey, tried the Continental practice of growing Turnips as a field crop in a 'Flanders rotation'. This took hold in the south east, and gradually spread beyond, despite Weston's work being published[20] for the whole nation to read. Thus it took until the 18th century for the new field crop to take hold in the north; first references for Northumberland are not until the 1720s.[21] Turnips do not succeed so well in the north anyway and the hill farmers did not necessarily have much arable land but a good thicket of Holly snuggled warmly between the hills could be a winter's salvation. Following the spread of Turnips and other root crops[22] came the decline in Holly fodder. It had served well, being known as wholesome Even as late as 1908 it was being listed as wholesome and productive of good milk and excellent butter.[23]

Although this section has concentrated upon farm animals, attention should be drawn to park animals – the deer in that opening list of beneficiaries. The deer parks were of course high status and therefore much depended upon the success of their herds, whether to provide venison or the sport of the chase. Both Red Deer and Fallow Deer will take Holly readily, as it is a natural part of their winter feed in the wild. Roe Deer are less keen but in times of want they will of course eat it.
(Red Deer illus. previous pages)

Finally, In complete contrast to the colourful spectacle of the royal hunt is this description of subsistence living, man and beast together, from the 13th century *Dream of Rhonabwy* from the Welsh *Mabinogion*[24]

"And as they came towards the house, they could see a black old hall with a straight gable end, and smoke a-plenty from it. And when they came inside, they could see a floor full of holes and uneven. Where there was a bump upon it, it was with difficulty a man might stand thereon, so exceedingly slippery was the floor with cows' urine and dung. Where there was a hole, a man might go over the ankle, what with the mixture of water and cow dung, and branches of holly a-plenty on the floor after the cattle had eaten off their tips."

---

[20] *Discourse of Husbandry.........*; 1645, enlarged 1651, corrected and enlarged again 1652 – by Samuel Hartlib. Weston's name does not appear as the author since he was not quite acceptable to all of Society, since he was a Roman Catholic recusant etc.

[21] Spray, p.102

[22] Sugar Beet and Mangel-wurzel increased the nation's options in the later 18th century.

[23] Dallimore, p.20

[24] from *The Mabinogion*, trans. G. Jones and T. Jones, 1949

HOLLIES IN THE GARDEN

BEGINNINGS

For hundreds of years Hollies have been grown in our gardens. It started, probably by accident, when medieval parks lost some of the house-side land to the creation of pleasure gardens and pre-existing trees were retained. Hedges were needed to keep out the park livestock and Holly had already demonstrated its ability to regenerate freely from being nibbled. Soon it was doing the same after clipping by the gardener. Back in Roman times the formal gardens were known as *topiarius*, according to Pliny, which became the title of the gardener responsible for them, according to Cicero, and from this we get *topiary* for trees and shrubs clipped into formal shape. Although Yew (*Taxas baccata*) and Box (*Buxus sempervirens*) are best known for this, Holly has been used as well. Often it is said that it was for Henry VIII (r.1509-47) that topiary was introduced into this country, and certainly he had 'animals' created in his influential park at Nonsuch Palace. However, John Leland, referred to topiary during mid reign so these must have been under creation at an earlier date. Today, topiary is back in fashion, even as potted specimens for patios. There is also renewed interest in the genus *Ilex* as the diversity between the species is re-appraised. The summaries here are for *Ilex aquifolium*, in keeping with the rest of the book.

HOLLY VARIETY

Just because the main Hollies used in Britain are from one species only plus one of its hybrids that does not mean there is little choice. There are over sixty cultivars of *Ilex aquifolium* ranging from plain green leaves to those edged or variegated with contrasting silvery cream through to rich gold.

The hybrid resulted from berries grown on after the tender Madeira Holly (*Ilex perado*) was stood outside in the summer of 1838 and its blossoms were fertilised by bees carrying pollen from *Ilex aquifolium*. That was at Highclere, Hampshire, thus the hybrid is known as the Highclere Holly, (*Ilex x altaclarensis*) although the same thing has happened elsewhere too.[25] Sadly examples of this basic cross are no longer known to exist.[26] There are numerous cultivars though and some of these, such as 'Golden King', are popular and common.

---

[25] Mitchell; *Pocket Guide....*
[26] according to Mitchell; *Field Guide.....*

The differences between the two are obvious once you know! The hybrid has broad flat leaves instead of the buckled leaves of Common Holly and that buckling forces the prickles out in several directions whereas the hybrid has the prickles facing forward and far fewer of them ('Wilsonii' has the most prickly leaves in this group). The hybrid also grows more robustly and the shoots are often flattened and can be purplish so that, all in all, good forms are readily distinguishable. There's always a tricky one though!

VARIEGATION

The great development in 20th century horticulture was for winter colour. The garden, for the first time, had to be attractive and inviting throughout the year, whereas in the days of the great gardener Gertrude Jekyll the winter was "the quiet time" and her attention focused upon natural evergreens:-

"Now the splendid richness of the common holly is more than ever impressive, with its solid masses of full, deep colour, and its wholesome look of perfect health and vigour. Sombrely cheerful, if one may use such a mixture of terms; sombre by reason of the extreme depth of tone, and yet cheerful for the look of glad life....." (1899[27]).

Thus there has been considerable interest in the variegated Hollies especially as they are indeed very attractive. For added interest is the variegated version of the Hedgehog Holly, 'Ferox', which has spines over the upper leaf surface as well as round the margins. It never fails to catch attention and the new shoots on the one in my garden are begged eagerly for Christmas decorations. That annual pruning has kept it to a three foot dome, from a rooted cutting I was given eighteen years ago. Once it has had some frostings the natural waxy surfaces become so reflective that even on bright but sunless days it looks as though the sun is shining on it. The colour contrast heightens too and with winter-flowering heathers around its feet is worth a couple of square metres of anyone's garden. Blue *Geranium* cultivars have crept in behind the heather and look good in summer so they're a tolerated accident, supplemented with shorter cultivars of dark foliaged red *Dahlias*. If the garden were being started again from scratch this would be one of the first acquisitions. This is one of the old cultivars; Parkinson described it back in 1640 (as *echinatum*) in his *Theatrum Botanicum*.[28]

PROPAGATION

Although readily available from garden centres the containerised specimens are often leggy, with their bottom foliage missing. That foliage is just what the tree grows to shelter the young bark from extremes of sunlight and frost. Furthermore, containerised plants can be pot-bound which the Holly takes several years to grow

---

[27] Jekyll, Gertrude; *Wood and Garden*; Longmans; 1899 but parts published previously in 1896-7 by *The Guardian* newspaper as "Notes from Garden and Woodland."
[28] pp.1486-7

52

out of, during which time that tight ball must be safeguarded from drying out. Of course there isn't a problem if it is intended to grow these on as potted features in the garden but if they are destined for the open ground the enthusiast is recommended to be a little more patient and start from cuttings! These should be heel cuttings taken from thin side shoots of about a finger's length but they take a long time to root so protect from winter weather in a cold frame; gentle bottom heat in a propagator will hurry things up a bit. Grow on in pots until well established but do not allow pot to fill with roots.

There is also the option of growing the seeds out of the berries. You may get a surprise because the male parent that supplied the pollen will influence the progeny – it may not be noticeable or you may get a new variation! Again, patience is needed. Seeds can take from eighteen months to over two years to germinate and during this time do not protect from frosts, which are needed to break the seeds' dormancy.

PLANTING OUT
Hollies will grow in most soils unless they are waterlogged. In the wild they can be an abundant understorey plant in open woodlands on acid sands, so this seems to be their favoured soil. On clay, add plenty of humus and this is even more important on chalk soils where a good mulch of compost each year will also be appreciated. The main problem is not so much the nature of the soil but keeping it from drying out, especially when overlying chalk and limestone, until the tree has got its root system well established. While it's doing that the top growth is slow, so be patient again. It's all very rewarding in the end.

Gardening book after gardening book will tell you Hollies are rock hardy and will come through any British winter unscathed. This is not so. Talk to country folk who remember long hard winters, such as 1963 when "even the hollies dropped their leaves" or 1947 when "it even killed our front hedge. Nice holly hedge we had." Prolonged cold in January, down to -12°C, does the damage, so if you garden in a frost pocket or at exposed high altitudes add plenty of other sheltering plants around your young Hollies. The infrequent hard frost seems to do little damage, unless it's in late spring and sears the new growth but recovery is rapid.

GETTING BERRIES

Don't despair if you want Holly berries but only have room for one tree and yet the books say you must have at least two – a male to provide the pollen and a female to bear the fruit. That is a general rule but there are exceptions. There are self-fruiting cultivars available, such as 'Pyramidalis' and 'J.C.van Tol' (also sold as 'Polycarpa'). Both have good green foliage to set off the berries. The latter has the brighter fruits and the darker leaves; indeed it can be such a blackish green that with careful siting it can become a significant feature but without care some may think it gloomy. Its stems are dark purple too whereas 'Pyramidalis' is one of the yellow-green stemmed group (and it has a yellow berried form 'Fructo Luteo')

Where there is room for more than one then different sexes can be chosen with perhaps the male being variegated to compensate for the lack of berries. Very popular is 'Silver Queen' which, despite being a queen is in fact male, just as the hybrid 'Golden King' is a female – one of horticulture's little peculiarities. Beware of using the Hedgehog Holly as a pollinator because, although male, the pollen is thought to be sterile so you won't get any berries. The lists on the opposite page are obviously not complete but are a selection for guidance only.

HEDGES

A hedge of Holly, Thieve that would invade,
Repulses like a growing palisade;
Whose numerous Leaves such Orient Greens invest,
As in deep winter do the Spring arrest.[29]

Protection, colour and tolerance of close clipping made the Holly familiar in the formal gardens of the Romans. It was recommended to them by Columella[30] and he must indeed have been influential since there were only four other complete books to which the Roman reader could turn for information on growing things.[31] In England the recommendation came through Fitzherbert's *Book of Husbundry* in 1523. The major influence came in 1662 with Evelyn's *Silva* and although Evelyn gets much credit where it isn't always due, when it comes to Hollies then he did indeed wax lyrical and write from personal experience. However, the following passage, famous as it is, gets misrepresented time and again:-

"is there under Heaven a more glorious and refreshing Object of the Kind, than an impregnable Hedge of about four hundred Foot in Length, nine Foot high, and five in Diameter; which I can show in my now ruined Gardens at Say's Court (thanks to the Czar of Muscovy) at any Time of the Year, glittering with its armed and varnished Leaves? The taller Standards at orderly Distances, blushing with their natural Coral: It mocks at the rudest Assaults of the Weather, Beasts, or Hedge-breakers."

[29] Couleii, Pl. 1.6; quoted by Evelyn, p.158
[30] Lucius Junius Moderatus Columella, mid-1stC. AD
[31] Harvey; *Medieval Gardens*; 21

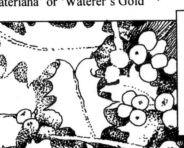

MALES
(*variegated and colour margined)
'Atlas'   green
'Crispa' or 'Contorta'   green
'Foxii'   green
'Golden Milkboy' *
'Golden Queen' or 'Aurea Regina' *
'Laurifolia Aurea' *
'Myrtifolia Aureomaculata' *
'Ovata Aurea' *
'Silver Queen' *
'Wateriana' or 'Waterer's Gold' *

Ilex x altaclarensis cvs
'Atkinsonii'
'Hodginsii'
'Jermyns'
'Maderensis'
'Mundyi'
'Nigrescens'

FEMALES
'Alaska'
'Amber'
'Aureo Marginata' *
'Argentea marginata' *
          plus a pendulous form
'Perry's Weeping Silver'
'Bacciflava' (yellow berries)
'Ciliata Major'
'Crassifolia'
'Fructo Luteo' (yellow berries)
'Green Pillar'
'Handsworth New Silver' *
'Madame Briot' *
'Pendula' pendulous habit
'Silver Milkmaid' or 'Argentea
          Media Picta' *
'Weeping Golden
 Milkmaid'   gold; pendulous

Ilex x altaclarensis cvs
'Belgica Aurea' or 'Silver Sentinel' *
'Camelliifolia Variegata' *
'Golden King' or 'King Edward VII' *
'Hendersonii'
'Howick' *
'James G. Esson'
'Ripley Gold'   gold variegated
'Wilsonii'
'W. J. Bean'

Firstly, let's get the location correct. Evelyn states quite clearly that the hedge is at Sayes Court. That was his London home, now lost under modern Deptford,[32] and is definitely not on the family estates at Wotton, Surrey, as can be found in print.

Secondly, the reference to the Tsar (Peter the Great) is constantly misconstrued. The Tsar did stay at Sayes Court, in the winter of 1698. Evelyn had made an arrangement through the Crown for the Tzar to stay there while enquiring upon shipbuilding at Deptford docks but Evelyn did not visit. He was then seventy eight and spending more and more time at Wotton, writing to friends that he had not only lost his teeth but was now losing some of his zest for life. It was a cold February and he preferred to stay by the warm fires at Wotton. Thus the hedge was not planted at the suggestion of Peter the Great during a conversation with Evelyn, as has been said. The hedge was already there. The popular story concerning this reference has Peter and his courtier, Menchikoff, taking it in turns to trundle each other around the grounds in a wheelbarrow, for fun, which occasioned great damage. Writers have since stretched this to the two of them flattening the hedge. Well, look at its dimensions; you can't flatten that with a wheelbarrow. The idea seems to come from the survey conducted by the King's gardener, George London, when Evelyn subsequently claimed for damages. George London lists damage to the grass walks and the bowling green, to a hundred feet of border-board [wooden edging to the formal beds], branches broken from fruit trees and so on. In particular he includes "*breaking Hollies and other fine plants*" and says three wheelbarrows were broken and lost.[33] It sounds as though it was young specimen Hollies that went under the wheel. Readers might like to know it wasn't just the outside that got wrecked but the interior too and 300 windowpanes; total damages paid by the Crown was £300.[34]

With increasing popularity of Holly for hedging at this time and into the early 18th century there was, inevitably, interest in the natural variations and variegated forms. The Hedgehog Holly (*Ilex aquifolium* 'Ferox') was known to Evelyn who thought George London had brought it out of France for the King. The accuracy of this has been questioned. Evelyn also records a white-berried Holly, which has been mentioned by other writers but now appears to be extinct. His yellow-berried cultivars are still available. The variegated Hollies were mixed in with the plain green; to see the effect, visit Wakehurst Place, Sussex,[35] where there is a section of golden variegated Holly in what is otherwise a Yew hedge.

---

[32] 0.9 hectares now a municpal park but not retaining Evelyn's original garden, except possibly an ancient Mulberry tree (inf. Lewisham Parks Dept.)
[33] Cal. Treasury Papers, 1698; details in Evelyn MS. 13, pp.485-6
[34] Cal. Treasury Books, 1697-8, p.360
[35] Admin. National Trust/Royal Botanic Gardens, Kew

There were several nurserymen from whom patrons could get their stocks of Holly. Among the most notable was a prominent gardener, William Darby (1677–c.1713) who ran a nursery as well, at Hoxton in London. There was also a Captain Foster at Lambeth who was known for his striped Hollies. Most important of all was the nursery of the Wrench family at Parsons Green Fulham, known for their range of variegated forms – "he gave rewards to people spotting remarkable kinds".[36]

At the same period the appreciation of Hollies spread to Scotland, particularly with the removal to Tyninghame in 1700 by Thomas Hamilton, 6th Earl of Haddington. There, in 1712, he planted long straight Holly hedges which attracted much attention.[37]

By the time the Victorians were arguing the various merits and demerits of the formal versus the naturalistic approach there were over a hundred different Hollies available. Collections were held by the great horticultural writers of the time, such as James Shirley Hibberd and William Robinson. The popularity of the tree persisted and many a provincial nursery held stocks. One was that of the Fletcher family at Ottershaw in Surrey. Their nursery lands covered 105 acres at one time and their boundaries were hedged with both green and variegated Hollies. Many sections survive today as a most unusual record. Dotted along these hedges are 'standards' just as Evelyn described three hundred years before. Holly hedges with standards have always been favoured – it is said in counties as far apart as Gloucestershire and Sussex that these are to unhorse witches as they speed through the night on their broomsticks using the hedges for navigation!

Ottershaw, Surrey – nursery boundary hedges now preserved along the roadsides

---

[36] Hadfield, p.11
[37] Hadfield; p.171

GARDENING FOR WILDLIFE

The gardens that attract the widest variety of wildlife are those that offer protection – from extremes of temperature, storms, icy winds, cats, birds of prey, and intimidating birds like Magpies. Holly can be an important component in any such garden. Its evergreen nature means it provides shelter throughout the year and at the same time filters wind, casts shade and helps to conserve moisture. They can be very valuable in difficult shady areas. If well positioned Hollies can make the garden look designed, structured and attractive to the householder too.

Many people would like more birds and butterflies in the garden but worry that a 'wildlife garden' might look a mess of weeds. This need not be so and hopefully the horticultural merits of the Holly will help dispel such beliefs. Then again there are those that think such a garden must have trees in it. That is not so but where trees of limited ambition are added (fruiting Rowans or Crab Apples for example) then Hollies can be planted underneath. This is their natural way to grow,

Painted Lady

tolerating broken shade and overhead dripping. They grow too slowly to be considered the *main* trees for most projects but as an understorey they thicken up the planting scheme and fill gappy draughty spaces. Leave some space though, probably a lawn, and then attractive little Dunnocks, will creep out from the Holly bushes to feed. They often do this when it starts to rain lightly; in my garden they have nested in Holly. Then there are the members of the thrush family that will come down to feed on fruit spread there, or flocks of starlings will probe for leatherjackets. Birds know the springing distance of a cat so make the space big enough and keep your Hollies and other bordering shrubs well back. It is the total habitat you create that will count most. Creating it out of a careful selection of plants will enhance it.

In terms of being attractive to wildlife, the Holly specifically is rather limited but protect them from rabbits and deer if they're among your gardening problems. The most noticeable beast is probably the leaf-miner that tunnels patterns through the thickness of the leaves. Otherwise you can look forward to feeding the birds with the berries (see berrying section above). Members of the thrush family – Blackbirds, Song and Mistle Thrushes, Redwings and Fieldfares – will all take Holly berries but will not be available in all gardens obviously. In some winters, especially if they are severe, the beautiful Waxwings may visit. In mild winters it is becoming increasingly common for some of our birds that have been considered summer migrants, such as the Blackcap, to now over-winter and these have been seen taking the berries.

*Spotted
Flycatcher*

Lastly there is a special butterfly, the Holly Blue. It is very small and so can be overlooked. For real success in attracting this you need to grow Ivy too and to let it grow up to flowering stage and then even a small patch of Ivy blooming in late autumn will attract the butterflies. The life-cycle of this butterfly requires you to grow both Holly and Ivy. There's nothing challenging in that!

THE MEDICINE TREE

Ever since ancient times Hollies have been used for treating bodily ills. Modern science would agree with some of these prescriptions, although it would most often turn to modern alternatives. Herbalism today has returned to the Holly. Some recommendations, however, appear to be based upon sympathetic magic, i.e. that its supposed sacred powers would make it particularly effective if taken into the body. This went further than the medicines themselves to include the belief that *any* medicines would be more effective if taken from a bowl made of Holly wood. This belief has persisted into living memory. That said, it is surprising perhaps that in our earliest medical texts, from late Saxon times, Holly plays no significant part, whether medicinal or through sympathetic magic. This is despite them containing much ritual healing through such things as charms. However, the Saxon texts embody knowledge, not only from far earlier periods, but also Classical material from the Mediterranean cultures where the Holly is not so well distributed. Thus there are only two recipes that have come down to us. The first comes from the *Lacnunga* manuscript, where those suffering from asthma are instructed to *boil holly-bark in goat's milk and sip it warm, having fasted.*[38] The second recipe is in *Book III* of the text known as *Bald's Leechbook*[39] which is based upon the lapidary of a Greek called Damigeron, working in Alexandria.[40] Recipe 69 reads:-

For if someone's stomach be soured and overswollen, take two large handfuls of holly leaves, shred them very finely, boil them in milk until they are thoroughly tender, pick it out piece by piece then let him eat six pieces, three in the morning and three in the evening after his food, do thus for nine nights, longer if it be needful to him.[41]

There was also a grand healing ritual performed with Ash trees but there are references to Holly being used as an alternative. Basically a child with internal injuries (described as 'ruptures' in old texts) was taken out to a sapling at the beginning of winter. The sapling was then split as it grew and the wood on either side of the split was pulled apart to create a magic loop. Through this the child was passed three times. Then the tree was bound up and left to heal. As it grew away strongly in the spring so should the child. This was still being practised in Italy in the early 1990s, where it had connections with rites of passage rituals. Another version was with loops of Bramble/Blackberry: 'the Poor Man's Mulberry' that gave rise to the rhyme *'Here we go round the mulberry bush'.* That version has been used well within living memory.

---

[38] from Pollington's trans. p.225
[39] Bald was the owner of the text, not the compiler; Pollington p.45
[40] Pollington, p.29
[41] from Pollington's trans., p.407

A glance into any of the old herbals will reveal a familiar list of complaints for which Holly was prescribed: bronchitis, chilblains, colic, diarrhoea, dropsy, fevers, fluxes, jaundice, rheumatism, stones, smallpox and warts. The important point to remember is that these entries are in printed herbals. In other words they are intended for the literate classes, who could afford to buy medicines. The vast majority of the population was not in that category so how they used Holly and for what conditions is known only fragmentarily. One exception, in that it is still very widely known today, (although few dare try it or need it!) is the treatment for chilblains which entailed thrashing them with sprays of Holly leaves (to increase the blood circulation). Most people seem to have opted for the alternative treatment of soaking their chilblained feet in a bowl of stale urine.[42]

Holly is used in some of the modern 'alternative medicine' treatments where, on the whole, it awaits official recognition. Of course many of these treatments have a beneficial effect on those who support them but when it comes to mental health things move slowly and are more difficult to assess. Nevertheless, some of the ideas link up with far older notions and may well prove valid. Selecting medicines that are appropriate to the patient's temperament is an ancient idea that is once again being taken seriously but when the respected Dr. Edward Bach started working the idea again in the 1920s and 30s he was very much a lone voice. Now the Bach Flower Remedies receive wide recognition, with Holly being used in connection with envy, jealousy, revenge, suspicion and vexation.

Caution should be exercised in the use of Holly for medicines. The tree contains toxins and not just in the berries. This causes concern for parents of young children if berried Holly is brought into the house. It need not be a major concern, for though the berries contain the toxins dihydromandelonitrileit and ilicin, they act as an emetic. Children who do consume any will vomit and rid their stomachs of the toxins. Some children only need a couple of berries to cause nausea but most can consume safely about twenty to thirty – at least, that is what the literature says up to 1899 but there has been no more recent evaluation. Apart from nausea, other symptoms are drowsiness and diarrhoea. The niceties were described in 1902 thus:

"The berries being strongly emetic in their action, came to his aid, and warned him not to do anything quite so foolish again, lest he became an awful example to the world at large, an interesting case in the text books, a tender memory to his sorrowing friends."[43]

---

[42] in medieval texts chilblains are 'kibes' or similar spelling.
[43] Hulme, p.160

THE PUB
CONNECTION

Numerous pubs are today called *The Holly Tree, The Holly Bush,* or simply *The Bush,* (as in the old music hall song *Down by the Old Bull and Bush*). The association arose out of the ancient Roman midwinter celebrations, where Holly symbolised the sun god and Ivy symbolised Bacchus, the god of ale and wine. Bacchus was depicted wearing Ivy in his long golden hair and/or a wreath of it around his head (said by some to be the origin of the Christmas wreath for hanging on doors). These two plants therefore became inextricably linked with alcohol. In 18th century Paris, for example, the vintner's shop was the one with Ivy painted up its doorposts and across the lintel, while in Britain the Holly prevailed. The choice of plants may well derive from their use in herbal treatments for drunkenness – an infusion from the chopped leaves of either, drunk straight down induced vomiting and thereby cleared the stomach of all excess alcohol. Don't try it though; remember it is toxic!

In Britain, alewives knew to their cost that simple home-brew does not keep well and it is imperative that the brew is sold quickly. Therefore, they needed a sign, for illiterate passers-by, to announce their fresh brew. A bush was nailed up over the door. It became customary for it to be a Holly, not just because of its alcoholic associations, unknown to the average passer-by, but because the Holly wouldn't wilt and go brown quickly as would other bushes.

Ancient Holly, near Speech House
Forest of Dean, 20.7.1995

This became ritualised in some places, as at Ashburton in Devon: *"On the Thursday of Carnival Week, which is held in Ashburton at the end of June or the beginning of July, the Ale Taster, together with the Portreeve and other officials, visits all the inns in the town to taste the beer and check on its quality. Originally, when about forty establishments in the town were brewing their own beer, it was to ensure that clean water and the right ingredients were being used. If the beer is deemed to be of acceptable quality, the Portreeve presents the landlord with a spray of evergreen to hang over his door."*[44]

SWEEPING THE CHIMNEY

Fireplaces with chimneys survive from Norman times[45] but it was not until the end of the Middle Ages that it was commonplace for them to have replaced the open fire in the centre of the hall floor. Once a building had a chimney there was the risk of the soot catching alight and house fires were common enough to impress upon people the need to keep the soot from building up in the chimney. One solution was to abrade the chimney with Holly.

Simply shoving a leafy bough up and down will do the job but is a foul job for anyone working in the hearth below. More effective is to use a whole young sapling with stiff side-branches radiating in all directions. By working from hearth and roof a short chimney could be cleaned but not the whole length of a taller one, even by tying the Holly on a rod and so for these a method employing ropes came into being. A bunch of holly was tied into the middle of the rope, or better still, two bunches tied in opposing directions to make a double-headed 'broom'. An operator on the roof dropped one end of the rope down the chimney to his partner in the hearth who then pulled down the slack until the Holly bunches were being dragged down the chimney. Once these reached the hearth it was the turn of the roofman to haul it back up again. Shunting it all up and down dislodged the soot. The rope enabled the hearthman to stand well back!

As the number of houses with chimneys proliferated from the 17th century onwards, so chimney sweeping developed into a familiar occupation and with it the practice of sending little children up the flues to abrade the brickwork by hand. Such children were bought cheaply from the workhouses that had a need to reduce costs upon the parish. Alternatively, children were bought off poor families for between twenty and thirty shillings for a seven-year apprenticeship. It was hardly

[44] Williams; p.29
[45] for the architectural development of these see Wood, Margaret; *The English Medieval House*; (1965); Bracken Books 1983.

that. The children were too big for the narrow flues after seven years, if they hadn't already got stuck and suffocated, or grown too deformed in the cramped conditions. They also developed cancers from the soot but before that stage many died from malnutrition. Sweeps saw little point in spending much money on food when children were so cheap and expendable.

That children should be considered cheap and expendable is an offensive idea today but only because of the changes in social attitude towards children. These were pioneered by the Victorians, who eventually outlawed the sweeps' 'climbing boys' and re-orientated Christmas into being child-centred with Holly now the central ritual plant. The plight of the sweeps' children was brought to public attention in 1773 by the London-based philanthropist, Jonas Hanway. He had already founded The Marine Society (1756) to rescue boys of good character from

18th and 19th century chimneys. Chertsey, Surrey, 1981 before site fire-damaged

street life to join the Royal Navy. That, however, was viewed as 'different' since it was at the start of the Seven Years War and therefore national security depended upon it. Interfering with the livelihoods of chimney sweeps was not a national concern. The limited response from Parliament in 1788 did not achieve the aims of the reformers. The next year William Blake published his *Songs of Innocence* and the arguments rambled on into the next century. Gradually public opinion did begin to change and action was taken on local levels. For example, *The Windsor and Eton Express*, reported that a petition against the practice had been received from Gloucester. So on 9th April 1818 a public meeting was held in the schoolroom at Staines "To take into consideration the propriety of abolishing the use of climbing boys and girls in sweeping chimneys". It was a quiet meeting, with those present concurring on the inhumanity of the practice, and resolving to dissuade local people from employing chimney-sweeping children. By that time George Smart had invented a mechanical sweeper which, it was said at the meeting, was "fully adequate".

Meanwhile, Parliament was still divided. In 1818 Lord Lauderdale led the conservative majority in the House of Lords with his view that, *"The better way, in judgment, would be to leave reforms of this kind entirely to the moral feeling of, perhaps, the most moral people, on the whole face of the earth."* Opponents, like Lord Shaftesbury, didn't find the situation at all moral but it took till 1840 to get another Act. It was ignored. Charles Kingsley published his *Water Babies* in 1863 and so there was another Act in 1864. This was also rendered ineffective *"by the callous connivance of private householders, local authorities, and magistrates".*[46] Finally, Lord Shaftesbury persuaded Disraeli's government to outlaw the practice totally, with the Climbing Boys Act of 1875.

It had taken over a hundred years to effect this change but it was a much broader issue. It was a revolution in attitudes towards children that created modern society. *"This enlarged sympathy with children was one of the chief contributions made by the Victorian English to real civilization. But such feelings were not universal, as the long delay over the chimney-sweep scandal testified."*[47]

During the long period of the climbing boys (and girls) special brushes and tools were developed and then mechanical means, leaving little record of the extent to which Holly was used. Probably not at all in urban areas of great demand but for an annual clean of a country farmhouse it was probably still employed. The last use known to me personally was in the early 1960s when an American took up residence in N.W.Sussex and enquired locally as to how to get the chimney swept. The locals, presumably with tongue in cheek, told him to cut a Holly off the common and do it himself. Much to their amusement he took them seriously and pronounced it very effective. An audience of 135 at an Over 60s Club in Surrey revealed 6.6% claiming they had swept chimneys with Holly in their lifetimes. (Feb. 2001)

---

[46] Hammond; *Lord Shaftesbury*; ch.XV
[47] Trevelyan, G. M.; *Illustrated English Social History*; Vol.4; p.158

A final note before leaving chimneys: any wooden beams that needed inserting within the heat of the fire were often of Holly due to its hardness. That made it fire resistant because the outside charred and thereby insulated the rest of the beam from the heat. This refers to such beams as those from which the pots were hung. An alternative choice of timber was Sweet Chestnut. Iron was often avoided because it can weaken in the heat and because the continual expansion and contraction could have adverse effects upon the chimney structure.

MAY DAY

Carried over from Part I, to keep themes more intact, is the ritual use of Holly by chimney sweeps as part of their May Day celebrations. This was one of their few annual holidays, and was when they went out into the daylight and sunshine to add to the street entertainment, as bands of actors and dancers and clowns. It began in the late 18th century, as did so much activity that we have been encouraged to believe is 'ancient tradition', and therefore its interpretations and supposed origins should be approached with extreme caution. It was described well by William Hone in his *Every-day Book, or Everlasting Calendar of Popular Amusements,* ' of 1825:-

Here they come! The 'sweeps' are come! Here is the garland and the lord and lady! Poor fellows! This is their great festival. Their garland is a large cone of holly and ivy framed upon hoops, which gradually diminishes in size towards an apex ....within it is a man who walks wholly unseen, and hence the garland has the semblance of a moving hillock of evergreens. The chimney-sweepers' jackets and hats are bedizened with gilt-embossed paper.....

Their lord and lady are magnificent indeed: he wears a huge cocked hat, fringed with yellow or red feathers, or laced with gold paper: his coat is between that of the full court dress, and the laced coat of the footman of quality....His lady is sometimes a strapping girl, though usually a boy in female attire, indescribably flaunty and gaudy; in her right hand a brass ladle....

When the garland stops, my lord and lady exhibit their graces in a minuet de la cour; in a minute or two they quicken into a dance....to the continued clatter of the shovel and brush held by each capering member of the sooty tribe. The dance concluded, my lord and lady interchange a bow and a curtsy; the little sootikins hold up their shovels, my lady with outstretched arm presents the bowl of the ladle. and 'the smallest donations are thankfully received' by all the sable fraternity.

THE WOOD AND ITS CRAFTSMEN

The qualities of Holly wood are not shared exactly with any other British timber. In summary, Holly wood is heavy, dense, close-grained, and nearly white. It polishes well and takes dye evenly. However, it must be seasoned properly or else it will warp and twist and split chronically. These characteristics have been known since ancient times, when Holly was used for spears and for the wheels and shafts of chariots. One of the most demanding roles it fulfilled was as pulley-blocks for ships' rigging; a demanding use because of possible extremes of temperature between voyages, constant wetting and drying and attack from salt spray. Some of the 'holly' wood available commercially today has in fact been imported from the United States and is *Ilex opaca* rather than our *I. aquifolium*.

Even before the timber leaves the felling ground some of it was used by the woodsmen themselves. Trees of all types used to be felled entirely with axes and wedges and for the latter the dense, close grain of the Holly was suitable and they can be made on the spot. The axe-man preferred to have his own collection of **wedges**, most of which were of hard seasoned heart of Oak. Some wedges in the woodsman's collection were of rarer timbers such as Box, Hornbeam and Yew. Beech was also used. Should rough mallets be needed out on site then they too were made from Holly, if available.

Cleaning up after felling a Holly saw the woodsman putting the spray on one side as **fodder, birdlime, Christmas decorations,** and **chimney sweeps' material** which are all reviewed elsewhere in this guide. Here, attention can be turned on **fuel** since the stems and branches were excellent for this. When it came to cutting up the lengths into logs the **sawing horse** itself was sometimes made of Holly.[48] Being dense the logs of Holly burn slowly, evenly and give off great heat. A log can be added to a fire while still green (i.e. unseasoned) and the heat boils the sap out. As a child this used to be scooped off with a finger and poked into aching ears (it worked,

---

[48] personal report from Sussex.

although the sap from Ash was better!). A traditional rhyme, found widely in varying forms round the country, tells us,

Holly logs will burn like wax
You may burn them green.

Indeed Holly was reckoned by many to be the finest fuel -*"a couple of holly logs on the Christmas fire will give a hotter fire than is possible with any other fuel".[49]* This may have extended to commercial use but it's very difficult to prove. It would seem unlikely, both from the point of view of the lack of knowledge of this and because the tree grows so slowly. Nevertheless, informants for the *Flora Britannica[50]* survey reported a correlation between Holly place-names in Lancashire and the proximity of tanneries, which was interpreted in terms of fuel.

Its fuel potential has been recognised since prehistoric times with the remains of Holly being found regularly by archaeologists in ancient hearth sites, whereby it becomes a valuable indicator of forest clearance.[51] Right through to modern times the woodland colliers have been more than happy to add it to their kiln stacks when making **charcoal**. No specific use for Holly charcoal was found when preparing *Trees, Herbs and Charcoal Burners*; it was just one of the broad-leaved trees that the colliers would use if it was found within the bounds of their cutting area.

In the domestic situation there was one drawback with using fresh green Holly and that is its tendency to 'pop' and shoot out burning splinters – not a good idea with rushes on the floor – nor hearth rugs! So familiar were the fierce burning qualities of this tree that it gets included in literary imagery, as in this ballad of *Earl Richard:-*

> *"The flame tuik fast upon her cheik,*
> *Tuik fast upon her chin,*
> *Tuik fast upon her fair bodye,*
> *She burned like hollins green."[52]*

Among the workers of the underwoods were those craftsmen who needed to split rods cut from coppice stools. Most frequently these were Hazel rods which were split into three. To achieve this, a three-sided wedge, called a **cleave**, was pushed through the length of the rod by the palm of the hand. Oak, Ash and Chestnut can and were all treated in the same way. Instead of a Holly cleave, one made of Box could be used if the craftsman could get one

---

[49] Arnold; p.239
[50] Mabey; p.248
[51] Godwin; p.173
[52] Child; Vol.III, p.153; stanza 29

The timber merchant then had a variety of outlets through which to seek sales of Holly timber. Attention is drawn to four of these: the block-maker, the bobbin-maker, the furniture-maker and the village woodworker.

THE BLOCK-MAKER
The dense close grain of a smooth block of Holly wood caught the attention of craftsmen who made printing blocks. They wanted something that could be pared away to leave raised designs that could be intricate without crumbling and didn't have the sort of fibres that would fluff up into a texture when wetted, didn't distort under pressure and would ensure an evenness of print. Such printing is a very old idea, found in ancient China for example, and was employed on both paper and cloth. In England, Holly has served this purpose for hundreds of years.

TEXTILE PRINTING
Textile printing really came to the fore with the industrial revolution that was spearheaded by the rapid development of a mechanised cotton industry. Clothing fashions changed dramatically from heavy wool to lightweight cotton. Wool needed any patterning to be woven into it at the time of manufacture, which was a slow and expensive business. Cotton cloth, however, could have designs printed on to it after weaving. This was not only cheaper but opened up a wider variety of designs and these could be far more intricate and had a new beauty all of their own.[53]

In the heyday of these blocks their prime use was for printing calico, a cotton cloth named after the city of Calicut in India from whence it was originally imported. That trade was in existence by the 11th century and printing the cloth was known by the 12th century. The term became used more widely to cover any plain or tabby white cotton cloth, while in American English it is applied to the cottons after they have been printed. The importation of the material is often said to have commenced through the trading of the East India Company in 1631 and the techniques for printing it were introduced in 1676. These dates do not tell the whole story, since calico type cloth was being exported from Calicut in our early Middle Ages which means it was being imported as a high status commodity into Norman England. Nevertheless, calicoes were an important fashion statement during the 17th and 18th centuries, in Britain and the rest of Europe. It was valued not only for costume but for hangings and bed covers as well, remembering that people entertained their guests from their beds! The imported cloth was usually plain and piece-dyed to give a ground colour upon which the designs were then printed.

---

[53] Trying to find such Holly blocks in use is nearly impossible today, but, having heard that a printing works in East London had been auctioned, it was possible to trace such blocks to their new owner at craft workshops in Hampshire. They were stained black from use and carried a Paisley design.

Originally such printing was done by hand but once the Industrial Age accelerated in Britain the process became mechanised. Britain led the world with its 'Industrial Revolution', with cotton at the forefront. This was concentrated in northern counties to the west of the Pennines, such as Lancashire. Those counties east of the Pennines, such as Derbyshire and Yorkshire, concentrated upon woollen cloth. These differences were due largely to the climate, since cotton fibres became brittle in dry conditions and difficult to work with the new machines. Lancashire, however, enjoyed a more humid airflow from the prevailing winds off the Atlantic. Thus calico gave rise to major centres of specialisation, such as Accrington. In 1831, Lewis's *Topographical Dictionary* described Accrington as:-

"a considerable village... Within the last few years this place has acquired considerable importance, from its situation in the centre of the calico printing business. Several large establishment for spinning cotton thread, and weaving and printing calico, have been formed, in consequence of which the population has increased nearly twofold."

Mass production of these cotton fabrics created a social revolution:- *"This was a revolution for ordinary people. Hitherto all materials had been expensive. Now there were fabrics that were available in great variety, often beautifully coloured or attractively patterned, costing the public a fraction of what had previously been paid."*[54] Costs had been high due, in part, to limitations in supply of the raw materials. There were greater limitations on the number of sheep that could be raised for wool and the number of acres that could be put down to flax for linen, than there were for cotton production in America. The British exchanged slaves for cotton in America[55] while back in Britain it was processed in the cotton mills under slave conditions that were no better. The emotive subject of the slave trade is likely to distract from the a social revolution in progress in Britain at the same time, namely the thousands of hand craftsmen who were being made redundant by the new machines, leading to the Luddite uprisings. A more personal view can be read in George Eliot's novel, *Silas Marner*. The handloom workers, as represented by the character Silas Marner would have encountered Holly as one of the prime materials from which their shuttles were made.

Cotton goods seemed limitless. They transformed dress, social etiquette, and personal hygiene for both men and women. The effects were seen and felt throughout the land, right down to the woodsmen who found a ready market for their Holly timber. The demand for Holly blocks must have been immense. Arguably this gave rise to the statement by C. P. Johnson in 1862 that *"In England the tree is usually small, rarely found growing to more than the size of a large bush, a circumstance partly to be accounted for by the value of the timber, which caused the larger trees to be felled in old times when wood of the kind was in greater comparative demand than at present."*

WALLPAPER PRINTING

If we could go back in time and look over the shoulder of a block-maker we would see a fine craftsman at work. In some workshops there would be teams of them, with the finest artist drawing out designs on to the wooden blocks. He might well work from a copybook in order to follow the latest fashions. These could include architectural designs, demanding geometry and symmetry, especially through the Gothic Revival of the 19th century. Once the drawing on the block was complete it would be passed to a carver with the skill to cut away the wood to leave the design standing proud. To cut round the contour lines was often a very intricate task and one that would hold the attention of a modern viewer. A more complicated situation arose when separate blocks were cut for every colour that would make up the complete design. This of course all added to the price and

[54] Ewing, p.60

[55] 1791 Britain transported 38,000 Africans to America – twice the total of other European participants. Ewing p.63

therefore to the status of its subsequent owner. In addition, there were taxes to pay on wallpapers until nearly mid-19th century and the ability to pay these became further statements of wealth. Then tastes changed:-

"Our ancestors would appear to have been of altogether tougher fibre than ourselves, judging by the amount of port wine that they drank, the wallpapers they could live with without flinching...." (Hulme. p.160)

BOOK ILLUSTRATION PRINTING

The same techniques were employed by a separate group of artist-craftsmen altogether. These were the people who produced woodcuts as fine-art illustrations. By the 15th century there were exponents of this art known to us by name and of lasting fame, such as Albrecht Durer (1471-1528). It is a very distinctive art that continued to maintain favour through the ages. It was not extinguished by the revolution in book production that came with the development of moveable type, nor by alternative techniques such as etching and engraving. Indeed England's most famous exponent wasn't born until 1753. He was Thomas Bewick. Much of his oevre is of small dimensions because it was only practical to use small blocks of wood, since he engraved into the end-grain. That is what has to be done to achieve high fidelity but it does mean a very hard, close-grained wood needs to be selected, such as Holly although artists declare Box is the very best.

Woodblock image, "Winter Fox" by George Taylor Reproduced with his kind permission

THE BOBBIN-MAKER

If we could go back in time and walk into the cotton mills during the Industrial Revolution we would find Holly wood in service on the looms and in the print works. The thread was spun onto large wooden bobbins and from these was woven into cloth. The bobbins were made by wood-turners and needed to be of a timber that would stay true so that they would rotate freely on their spindles. Failure to do this would snap the thread and halt production. Similarly, the timber needed to be one that would have such a hard smooth surface after turning that there was no texture to snag or wear the thread. Holly was ideal. In 1802 the demand for these from the Lancashire mills required the felling of 150,000 Holly trees.[56] It is difficult to imagine that these bobbins rotating on their spindles would wear out very quickly, to need replacement, so much of this demand must have been for the equipping of new machines as the industry continued to expand. However, if demand put pressure on supply then wood-turners may have worked the Holly before it was thoroughly seasoned. Then the bobbins might well warp out of true and not rotate freely. That would require their replacement.

THE FURNITURE-MAKER

By the 16th century there had been considerable enhancements to medieval house design that encouraged the development of furnishings. Out of this arose the technique of **inlay** work, whereby strips of pale wood were embedded in thin grooves cut in dark work so as to create contrasting patterns. Holly was one of the woods chosen for this. It was also used as an underlay for thin plates of ivory "to render it more conspicuous."[57] Obviously this section applies to high status homes, not the village homes on the manor.

Tudor rooms, in the wealthiest homes, had small-paned windows and wood-panelled walls so they were dark, by our standards. This is how they liked things, so the furniture was often stained dark too. Natural Oak was blackened with dyes or more cheaply with lamp black or soot. Polished edges reflected candle and lamp light to create luminous lines of design through the mouldings and turned balusters. Soon these bright lines became a constant feature, in whatever light, by the use of inlays, which inevitable developed from straight lines into curvilinear patterns. From a social history viewpoint the important issue here is the display of wealth to impress visitors.

The obvious furnishing to deserve this refinement, to impress visitors, was the table. However, by this time, it was the norm to display wealth by covering the table with expensive linen tablecloths that had their own etiquette for the side falls.

---

[56] Nicholls, P. H.; *On the Evolution of a Forest Landscape*; in Trans. Inst. of Brit. Geography; 1972; p.56

[57] Evelyn, 161

In other words, the inlays would be hidden from view. A visitor's eye, however, went not so much to the table as to the furnishing nearby from which the expensive tableware had been delivered. It was basically a cupboard, sometimes raised to allow room for a pot-shelf below, but definitely with display shelves above. Thus to modern eyes it looked like a *dresser* and indeed in the inventories can sometimes be found listed as such, although that word was used more often for a piece of kitchen furniture. *Cupboard* appears in the lists and in today's reference books these are likely to be referred to more specifically as *court cupboards*. At this time the French term *buffet*, comes into use but soon becomes used for a different style of cupboard altogether. Such furnishings became popular during the first part of the 17th century but declined during the last quarter of the century as fashions changed.

The early ones were about four feet wide and six feet tall and the cupboard should contain, ideally, gold and silver plate. It revealed the host's wealth and therefore his status, so rules of etiquette developed. A knight should only have one shelf but a duke could have five. Cardinal Wolsey's drew comment because it had six shelves and that broke the rules but then Cardinal Wolsey considered himself above censure! His king, Henry VIII, had eight shelves of course! It must have been very impressive when the gold and silver was all set out, gleaming in the light of two special candles, large ones of course; they were expensive too. Apparently all this display was tempting too, since some had railings round them to keep admirers beyond arm's reach! Best of all was when a very wealthy host could show these items were surplus to requirements by serving up hospitality on another set! This had to be of just as high a quality so as not to insult the guests.

Whereas inlays were set *into* the surface there soon developed the technique of cutting small pieces and setting them in patterns *on* the surface between sections of veneer. This technique came from abroad, with the French name *marquetry* or *marqueterie*. Again Holly was used, not only for its own whiteness but also stained or dyed to imitate other, more expensive woods, such as Ebony. Soon craftsmen were working with larger pieces. Sometimes geometric designs were elaborated into architectural scenes. Alternatively they produced amazing floral studies, akin to the Dutch still-life paintings. Influences came from the Continent, from the Low Countries and from the Palace of Versailles. It inevitably offended some of the conservative English, like John Evelyn, who looked back with nostalgia to the days of simple, sturdy, English oak furniture! He thought the adoption of foreign styles and materials was *"corrupting ancient simplicity"*.[58] He was in the minority though; marquetry became extremely popular. There were revivals of the geometric patterns and these were differentiated by the term *parquetry*. Where this creates a mosaic border the term *English Mosaics* is often applied. A table in the 1851 Great Exhibition had over 100,000 pieces.

---

[58] preface to *Mundus Muliebris*

Of note, in this context, are the items that are known as *Tonbridge Ware*, after Tonbridge in Kent[59]. Here the 17th century styles and skills were revived in the early 19th century.[60] Foremost among these craftsmen was the family of Wise who had their premises next to the Medway Bridge in the town. They developed the style to the point where they were including engravings into the design. They made their own engravings and hand coloured them before protecting with a glazing of varnish. Subjects ranged from a view of Tonbridge church to the fashionable places of the day, such as the seaside resorts of Brighton and Margate.

The chief products were boxes. The Victorians loved boxes – for artists' paints, cigarettes, cribbage, gloves, jewels, keys, money, playing cards, spices, trinkets, stamps, tea, etc. Among the larger furnishings of note is a folding table made for Prince Albert by Fenner & Co. in 1845.[61]

Another furnishing that contained Holly was the harpsichord, and it still does today when possible. Tiny chips are included in the structure of the jacks, for the plucking of the strings. Only such a hard wood as Holly can be cut to such tiny proportions without crumbling. Some of course have lasted hundreds of years.

---

[59] some books spell this Tunbridge after nearby Tunbridge Wells
[60] although the last craftsman is listed as Thomas Green at Rye in Sussex in the 1930s
[61] now in Kensington Palace

THE VILLAGE WOODWORKER

To enter the shop of the village carpenter or wood-turner could well have been facilitated by Holly since it seasoned hard enough to use for **door furniture**, such as for door bars and bolts and *"they made even Hinges and Hooks to serve instead of Iron."*[62] The tools on the bench could well have Holly **handles**.[63] This use was widespread, from Evelyn's records from Surrey to Darwin's for Scotland.[64] The wood is dense enough to resist splitting when struck by the mallet and it wears to a wonderful smooth surface for comfort in the palm of a hand.

Small cutting tools held that way were used for fashioning small **carved items,** such as **snuff boxes** which were fashioned out of the knots and burrs of the tree trunks. Another example would be the heads for the knights pieces in a **chess** set, when the whole set could be of Holly, left plain for the 'white' pieces and stained for the 'black' pieces. Most of the work to produce chessmen (32 per set) was done on the lathe. They weren't turned individually but several, such as eight pawns, were worked at a time, joined top to bottom, from a single length of wood. This was mounted between the centres of the lathe for spindle turning. Once complete, the pieces were cut free. Another technique, to be seen nowadays at wood-turners' demonstrations, was to create loose rings still trapped round the spindle of wood from which they were cut, making thereby a **baby's rattle**. Holly was ideal for this since, not only because it was smooth and splinter free but because it would not release stain or toxins into the baby's mouth. One of the bigger jobs was turning Holly into **bowls**, especially when these were worked as a set with one inside the other so as not to waste the core. Holly bowls, although devoid of graining, can be quite beautiful in their simplicity, with the dense grain giving them a cold marble-like finish. A very different product is the **billiard cue**, which has had its butt made of Holly. Today there are specialists for the manufacture of these but that was not the case when the game was introduced from the Continent back in the 15th/16th centuries. Another specialist, from older times, was the **fan** maker, using Holly for the pale handles of hand-held fans, once so fashionable with the ladies in their printed cotton dresses.

Spoons, plain or carved, but usually plain for kitchen use, were most often made of Holly or Sycamore (*Acer pseudoplatanus*) for their whiteness – the importance of hygiene in the kitchen has been understood since Elizabethan times even if the existence of germs was unknown. Indeed, Holly and Sycamore were the chosen timbers of one of England's last spoon-makers, at King's Cliff, Northants, whom Edlin described at work thus:-

---

[62] Evelyn. p.161
[63] Edlin. p.118
[64] Darwin. p.72

"He trimmed his logs on a paring block with a quaint hinge paring knife, and then cleft out spoon blocks. Each of these was then fixed in a groove at one of a low stool, whereon the carver sat to chip out the spoon bowls with a quaint adze; this tool had a curved and weighted blade, and an extra handle set at right angles to the main shaft. The hollow was smoothed out with a curved knife like that used in Wales, whilst another sharp-pointed knife was used to shape the outside of the bowl, and the whole spoon was then set in a lathe to turn its straight round handle." [65]

A much bigger job was making **coffins**. These only came into general use in the 17th century, instead of burying in a shroud. Holly was rarely used because the large planks needed were in demand for other purposes. A more specialised job was the making of **mathematical instruments**, utilising the paleness to show up the calibrations and the hardness to resist distortion; obviously the timber must be very well seasoned for this purpose.

Ancient Holly by the Speech House, Forest of Dean, 20-7-1995

---

[65] Edlin, 79

SELECTIVE BIBLIOGRAPHY

Aubrey, John; *The Natural History and Antiqities of the County of Surrey*;
    1718-19 (rep. Kohler and Coombes, Dorking, 1975)
Beckett, Kenneth and Gillian; *Planting Native Trees and Shrubs*;
    Jarrold, Norwich, 1979.
Bower, F. O.; *Botany of the Living Plant*; MacMillan; 1956
Brimble, L. J. F.; *Trees in Britain*; MacMillan; 1948
Coles, William, *Adam in Eden*, 1657
Dallimore, W.; *Holly, Yew and Box, with notes on other Evergreens*;
    John Lane The Bodley Head; 1908
Darwin, Tess; *The Scots Herbal: The Plant Lore of Scotland*;
    Mercat Press, Edinburgh; 1966
Edlin, Herbert; *Woodland Crafts in Britain*; Country Book Club;
    Newton Abbot; 1974
Evelyn, John; *Silva: or a Discourse Of Forest-Trees*; 5th ed. used; 1729
    Ewing, Elizabeth; *Everyday Dress 1650-1900*; Batsford; 1989
Gloag, John; *A Short Dictionary of Furniture*; Allen and Unwin; 1952
Freke, Timothy and Gandy, Peter; *The Jesus Mysteries*; Thorsons; 1999
Godwin, Sir Harry; *History of the British Flora: a Factual Basis for*
    Phytogeography; CUP; 1984
Hadfield, Miles; *A History of British Gardening*; Penguin; 1985
Hammond, P. W.; *Food and Feast in Medieval England*;
    Wrens Park Pub. 1993
Harvey, John; *Early Nurserymen*; Phillimore; 1974
    Medieval Gardens; Batsford; 1981
Hervey, Thomas; *The Book of Christmas*; 1888
Howkins, Chris; *Dairymaids Flora*; Chris Howkins pub. Addlestone; 1994
Howkins, Chris and Sampson, Nick; *Searching for Hornbeam*;
    Chris Howkins pub. Addlestone; 2000
Hulme, F. Edward; *Wild Fruits of the Countryside*; Hutchinson; 1902
Hutton, Ronald; *The Stations of the Sun: A History of the Ritual Year*
    in Britain; OUP; 1996
Jekyll, Gertrude; *Wood and Garden*; Longmans; 1899
King, John; *The Celtic Druids' Year: Seasonal Cycles of the Ancient Celts*;
    Blandford; 1994
Lowson, J. M.; *Textbook of Botany*; University Tutorial Press; 1962
Mabey, Richard; *Flora Britannica*; Sinclair-Stevenson; 1996
Michell, Alan; *A Field Guide to the Trees of Britain and Northern Europe*;
    Collins; 1992
    The Pocket Guide to Trees of Britain and Northern Europe;
    Dragon's World Ltd; 1992.
Parkinson, John; *Theatrum Botanicum*; 1640
Pollington, Stephen; *Leechcraft: Early English Charms, Plant Lore,*
    and Healing; Anglo-Saxon Books; 2000
Radley, J.; 'Holly as a Winter Feed' in *Agriculture Historical Review*;
    Vol IX; pp.89-92; 1961
Royal Horticultural Society; *Dictionary of Gardening*; MacMillan; 1992
Spray, Martin; 'Holly as a Fodder in England' in *Agriculture Historical Review*;
    Vol 29; pp.97-110; 1981
Trevelyan, G. M.; *Illustrated English Social History*; Pelican; 1964
Williams, Michael; *Superstition and Folklore*; Bossiney Books; St. Teath,
    Cornwall; 1982

INDEX

For list of other books dealing with the social history of trees write to the publisher's address on page 2.